BUG FIGHTERS

A History of Dow AgroSciences, 1897-2007

For two old friends –

Keith C. Barrons (1912 – 2003), who had the original idea for this book and did much of the research for it, and

H. D. (Ted) Doan (1922 – 2006), who insisted that this book had to be written and provided the leadership and support that brought it into being.

BUG FIGHTERS

A History of Dow AgroScience, 1897-2007

Part I. BEGINNINGS

Part II. GROWING UP

Part III. THE MODERN ERA

SOURCES AND ACKNOWLEDGMENTS

One fine spring day in 1993 a long-time friend came by to visit us at the headquarters of the Herbert H. and Grace A. Dow Foundation in Midland, Michigan. He was Keith Barrons, one of the truly remarkable trail-blazing pioneers of the Dow agricultural chemical business. He told the author and Ted Doan, then president of the foundation, that he would like to become a consultant to the Foundation and its affiliate, the Post Street Archives. In his retirement years, he said (he was then 81 years old), he had been collecting odds and ends of the history of the Agricultural Chemicals branch of Dow, with which he had then been associated for more than 50 years, through and from old friends and colleagues in the organization. He proposed to continue this task, which he greatly enjoyed, but he felt he needed some sort of official or unofficial status to make his work "legitimate".

As a consultant to the Foundation, he proposed, he would continue to collect materials and documents and "write-ups" from his old "aggie" friends, and turn them over along with his own "write-ups" to the Post Street Archives.

All he wanted in return for this was his expenses (his telephone bill, he said, was "out of sight"), and a blushingly modest stipend. These details were quickly agreed upon, and for the next 10 years, until his death at 91, Keith Barrons worked diligently and faithfully at his appointed task, visiting the Archives two or three times a year to discuss his work. Kathy Thomas at the Archives typed up and organized the material as he produced it.

The result was what are called the "Keith Barrons Papers", now housed at the Post Street Archives. They became the single most important resource for the writing of this volume, which is designed to be a general history of farming chemicals over the past century or so as seen through the optics of one of the key companies in that field, The Dow Chemical Company. The Barrons papers constitute what is surely one of the most complete and expertly fashioned historical records of an agricultural chemical company in existence, put together with loving care and pride by one of the central participants in that history.

1

The author first and foremost therefore must acknowledge his indebtedness to Keith Barrons, and also to Ted Doan; who encouraged and vigorously supported this entire enterprise, except in its final stages. When Keith died in 2003, Ted told me, "Well, now you'll just have to write the book yourself. We'll have to finish what we started". Sadly enough; Ted himself died in 2006, before the work was completed.

Wherever you are, Keith and Ted, here it is.

We also need to acknowledge the assistance provided by the many volumes of oral history that have also served as primary source material, as listed in the appendix. They were made in this same period of time, and supply much valuable information concerning the main protagonists of our story. In most of these my co-worker and partner was Prof. James J. Bohning of Lehigh University, and I am once again grateful for his expertise, and his friendship. This is the third volume of Dow Chemical Company history that has relied on these oral histories for accuracy and authenticity. Dr. Arnold Thackray, president of the Chemical Heritage Foundation, Philadelphia, Pa., and our mentor in the oral history field, has been a valued and valuable counselor throughout the process.

The Herbert H. & Grace A,. Dow Foundation has graciously funded the oral history program from its inception twenty years ago, and I express once again my appreciation to Margaret A. (Ranny) Riecker, president, and Jenee L. Velasquez, executive director, for their generous and faithful support.

The staff of the Post Street Archives, especially its director, Tawny Ryan Nelb, and Kathy Thomas, its librarian for most of this period, Delores Goulet, photographic archivist (and an old "aggie" herself), Connie Good, Kathy McCormick, and Christina (Chrissy) Westbury, have all been unfailingly helpful. The Archives hold virtually all of the materials presemtly available concerning the history of the Dow AgroSciences organization, and I was fortunate to have complete access to these records.

Finally, there must be noted the individual contributions of a great many of the old "aggie" veterans themselves, who cooperated and volunteered and assisted with this project in so many ways. Cleve Goring contributed various basic reference books from his library, and resource materials concerning the history of the Seal Beach and successor ag chemical laboratories in California and the American West, including a copy of an invaluable history of the development of ag chemical products in that region written by John F. Kagy.. Gene Kenaga provided materials concerning his exemplary service as the company's first ecologist. Etcyl Blair provided materials from his long and intimate experiences with the dioxin controversy.

I thank them all. As a postscript, I must apologize to those "aggies" whose activities and accomplishments are not discussed in this work. It would take a big fat several-volume encyclopedia to include them all, and I have had to pick and choose. That is one of the basic conundrums of the historian -- having to pick and choose those events that in his or her estimation constitute the main lines of an organization's history. We cannot be all-seeing or all-inclusive, much as we would like to be. Many of the events and projects that have been omitted, I agree, are surely worthy of the historian's attention. Perhaps another historian will treat them, and you, more kindly in another age.

E. N. (Ned) Brandt

June 29, 2007

    Midland, Michigan

A NOTE ABOUT NOMENCLATURE

Before we begin exploring the history of farm chemicals there is a problem we need to discuss, and that is the question of nomenclature.

Most of the farm chemicals we will be discussing have three separate and distinct names, and some of them have even more.

First of all, they have a chemical name. This is commonly long and complex, and doesn't trip off the tongue easily, so it is seldom used except by specialists. Take, for example, 0,0-diethyl-0-(3,5,6-trichloro-2-pyridinol) phosphoro-thioate, the chemical name for what became for a time the world's top seller in the insecticide field.

This is a tongue-twister even for graduate chemists, so the substance is usually referred to by its second name, chlorpyrifos, a few syllables plucked out of the chemical name (and simplified a bit) -- chlor - pyri - phos. This is its common or generic name.

And third, the same substance has a trade name, that is, a brand name attached to it by its manufacturer. In our example, the substance was discovered by Dow Chemical, and introduced to the world by the Dow brand name, Dursban. It also has the name of Lorsban in its agricultural applications. And if some other company purchases chlorpyrifos from Dow and uses it as part of a compound it can give it its own brand name, as long as it indicates that chlorpyrifos is the active ingredient.

By whatever name, it's all the same substance. Pharmaceuticals, by the way, follow the same sort of naming system, and both of these disciplines have done so since roughly the end of World War II.

Please note also that the trade or brand name is always capitalized -- Dursban, Lorsban -- and that the common or generic name -- chlorpyrifos -- is never capitalized.

During the early period covered by this volume (Part I -- 1897-1939), which was what may be termed the inorganic period -- almost all the farm chemicals of that time were inorganic chemicals -- the nomenclature rules were much looser. No common or generic name was required, and one might be used, or might not. A product based on lead arsenate, for instance, would simply be called by the name of the maker and the principal ingredient -- Dow Arsenate of Lead. When Dow's first organic pesticide -- it was a mite control compound, dinitro-o-cyclohexyl phenol -- was introduced, it was called DNOCHP. Designation by the product's chemical initials was for years a popular practice.

Dinitro-o-sec.butyl phenol, a herbicide, for example, was called DNOSBP in early sales literature but was later given the common name "dinoseb" (from DNOSB, of course), and dinoseb it has remained. Dow General Weed Killer and Dow Selective Weed Killer were formulations incorporating dinoseb as the active ingredient.

Since about the end of World War II, when these naming methods became accepted practice, pesticides have had a common name designating the active ingredient, plus one or more trade names for specific products containing that active ingredient. Dow's first pyridine-related herbicide, for instance, was assigned the common name, picloram, derived from the chemical name -- 4-amino, 3,5,6-trichloro-picolinic acid. The first trade name assigned to the compound was Tordon, and products containing Tordon had varying names. Tordon 101 Mixture, for instance, contained picloram and 2,4-D. Internally at Dow, Tordon was sometimes used as if it were another name for the active ingredient, picloram, rather than a formulation of it, and employees referred to the plant as "the Tordon plant", rather than "the picloram plant". It was "the Dursban plant" rather than the chlorpyrifos plant. This came about because Tordon and Dursban were the first and most important products containing picloram and chlorpyrifos.respectively.

This loose way of using a trade name very likely came about because in the product introduction stage more than one product containing the active ingredient was marketed, and sometimes several. For instance, dalapon (common name), the grass killer which is chemically 2,2-dichloro-propionic acid, was introduced as Dowpon for farm use and as Radapon for industrial use.

This system for choosing a name for a new product grew out of the requirement that the introducer of a new product had to register the active ingredient with the Federal registration agency, suggesting a name for the new product when doing so. Before 1970 this registration agency was the U.S. Department of Agriculture, and since then it has been the Environmental Protection Agency. For a while the professional societies had a role in the naming process -- the Weed Society of America had a hand in the naming of herbicides, for example -- but while this worked well in some cases, in others it did not, and the practice was abandoned. Registration by the EPA now makes a product name official. Trade names for products are usually also registered with the U.S. Trade Mark Office.

Basically, in sum, what you need to know is that there are three names for most farm chemical products -- the chemical name, the common name, and the brand name -- and that we will be dealing almost exclusively here with the common or brand name.

A PROLOGUE: The "Aggies"

Alexis Millardet, the French botanist, is a forgotten man today, but a century ago he was one of the heroes of the hour, the inventor of Bordeaux mixture, the first agricultural fungicide. The generally accepted story is that a grape grower in Millardet's neighborhood, the Bordeaux wine region of France, was having trouble with teen-age boys stealing his grapes, and was trying to devise a way to prevent this. One day he mixed up some crystals of blue copperas with lime and water, and splashed it on his grapes, giving them an odd light blue color which he thought might deter the boys, or at least get them to pilfer grapes from someone else. He discovered something totally unexpected, however. The grapes he splashed with this mixture were entirely free of downy mildew, a fungus that plagues grapes.

Among those he told about his discovery was Millardet, and Millardet, immediately intrigued, set about conducting some experments. Three years later, in 1885, he announced the discovery of Bordeaux mixture, as it is called, a 3:1:100 mix of copper sulfate, calcium oxide, and water. For the next half-century or so Bordeaux was used in French vineyards and around the world to fight mildew (in French, mildiou) in grapes and other crops.   Millardet is given credit for saving the French wine industry by conquering a disease that threatened to destroy it.1

The impact of bug fighters such as Millardet and his successors on our lives is a subject
that has been widely ignored. In the pages that follow we are going to buck that trend and tell you the stories of a variety of such fighters. Their lives and discoveries are scattered across the 20th century, during which timeframe humankind made almost miraculous progress in its battle against the bugs -- they being the assorted thousands and thousands of varieties of worms, insects, aphids, mites, fungi and assorted other critters that assail our food crops.

In the century just past we humans finally began to learn how to deal with these creatures in an effective way, and it can now be safely said that man has finally conquered his insect foes.

Man has won this battle.

So in this volume we will celebrate some of the people who made this possible, who call themselves "aggies". This is not a general history of farm chemicals. It is the story of how one of the major agroscience firms came to be and to grow into one of the world's largest firms of its type, based from the beginning on the research and development of products designed to control the depredations of the bugs.

The bugs represent an almost overwhelming challenge, to start with. More than one million species of insects have been described for us by those who study them, and they constitute about 75 per cent of all the species in the animal kingdom.   Some 100,000 plant diseases are known in North America alone, and while not all of them are important, a great many are. Some 8,000 species of fungi, 500 of nematodes, 250 of viruses and 160 of bacteria cause significant diseases of our economic crops.   On a crop basis 115 diseases are reported on tomatoes, 160 on potatoes, 77 on wheat, 112 on corn, and 200 on apples.2

The stories that follow detail the attacks on some of the more important of these predators.

It is one of the triumphs of modern science. Man has now, finally, after all these centuries, conquered his rivals and arch-enemies for the foodstuffs a bountiful nature has provided him, and we can now declare a victory in this age-old battle.

It is recorded that the Egyptian pharaohs of five thousand years ago put slaves to work picking insects off their growing crops, but they were only the first to use such primitive (and generally speaking, ineffective) methods. Over the centuries various kinds of magic, smoke and incense and prayers were used against the pests, and incantations and sacrifices to the gods. None of it worked very well.

Others of the ancient races tried more esoteric devices such as dancing naked through their fields under the beneficent rays of the full moon, to the accompaniment of priests blowing horns and beating drums.. This display did not bother the insects and their kindred overly much, and they continued to munch away on the crops in spite of such distractions.

In the meantime famine and drought and starvation have been regular visitants to planet earth from time immemorial. As recently as 1921 the headlines said that an entire modern nation, Russia, was starving to death. "No one can count the victims", one account said, "but some seven million people may have died from hunger and disease since the Bolshevik Revolution...The worst-hit area is the huge Volga region east of Moscow where people are eating clay and twigs and cannibalism has appeared"..3

This was still, incredibly, an improvement over the pre-Bolshevik record in Russian history. In 1907 alone, it is estimated, 20 million people starved to death in Russia "in the worst famine on record". 4

Asia and Africa have been the most frequent arenas for these disasters. In 1878 it was reported that "over five million prople have died of famine in the Deccan (i.e., central) area of India in the past two years". A year later uncounted millions were reported dying in China in a three-year famine that was "one of the most terrible famines ever visited on this troubled country....the crops have failed. The fields have turned to dust. Even the thatch from roofs has been eaten. Good work is being done by the missionaries, but the disaster is too vast. Hunger triumphs".5

Famine is, of course, a phenomenon usually brought on by extreme weather factors, principally long droughts. These events may also be insect- or pest-related, dating back to the plagues of locusts described in the Bible. At other times both weather and insect pests were factors, as in the famous potato famine in Ireland in 1846, when drought and potato blight combined to destroy the potato crop in its virtual entirety and millions of Irish perished. (Many of those who survived were inspired to migrate, principally to the United States and Canada).

These plagues of drought and locusts, and the rest of it, continue even today. In August 2005, for example, the news services reported an invasion of locusts and a drought in Niger, "the second-poorest nation in the world, where 64 per cent of the people survive on less than $1 a day". "Last year locusts, in the worst invasion in 15 years, ravaged 7,000 square miles of Niger farmland" this report said. "Today, more than a third of the nearly 12 million people in Niger face severe food shortages. Children are most at risk". "Nearly 4,000 villages across Southern Niger need help", another report said, because of "Niger's worst nutrition crisis since 1985".6 The locust, a short-horned grasshopper, is probably the most difficult of these creatures to fight against, being "a migratory grasshopper often traveling in vast swarms and stripping the areas passed of all vegetation".7 Heaven help the people of Niger.

But let's look at the other side of the ledger.

Dr. J. V. Jacks, a British soils specialist, studied the yield of wheat per acre in Great Britain from 1100 A.D. to the present time, and his findings offer an illuminating view of the increases in crop yield that have occurred over the long view of history. In 1100 the wheat yield in Britain was about five bushels per acre, and it held steady at that figure until about 1350 A.D., until by 1500 A.D. the yield had climbed to 10 bushels per acre, and it then climbed very gradually again until 1900, when it reached 15 bushels per acre. In the 20th century it moved up very rapidly, to 28.4 bushels per acre in 1938-40, to 78.0 bushels in 1968-70, to 92.2 bushels in 1971-73.8

Thus, the wheat yield increased only very gradually for eight long centuries, from 1100 to 1900 and then spiraled upward at a dizzy pace in the 20th century.

What happened? Most experts agree that there were five principal factors involved:

    1. Genetically improved varieties and hybrids became available to the farmer -- things like hybrid corn, "miracle" rice, dwarf Mexican wheat.

    2. Improved management -- increased knowledge of soils, irrigation, and plant responses to their environment.

    3. Better plant nutrition, especially the mineral nutrition of plants and the developments that brought about the large-scale production and availability of fertilizers.

4. Control of pests, including the development of genetic resistance to many diseases, and the control of insect and other pests through crop protection chemicals.

5. Farm mechanization -- modern machinery that facilitates everything on the farm from irrigation to planting to harvesting to crop protection.9

In the 21st century instances still occur in which man fights his insect foes with drum-beating and incantations, but by and large these ancient practices have been abandoned in favor of a more scientific approach. This book will introduce you to some of the people who carry on the combat against the pestilential species. It will not introduce you to all of them, for there are too many, but to a sampling of the various kinds of people who devote their lives to the battle against man's food pests. These people are truly, as our title suggests, "Bug Fighters". Their battles are waged against the insects and pest species who compete to devour the food output of the world.

The "Bug Fighters" treated in these pages are but a tiny part of their confreres across the world. They have been selected as representatives of the international forces that wage this battle. Many other representative could of course have been chosen. The fighters whose careers are sketched here, all of them employees of the same company, have been conspicuously successful in the fight, and their accomplishments over the past 100 years are typical of the more successful combatants in other companies, in other countries, around the world.

At the same time, those selected have played some historical role in the conflict, and as a whole, their stories make up a general history of the battle against the insects during the past century or so.

Dow AgroSciences, as the firm is called today, is only one of the many companies waging this battle around the world, and its history has been paralleled by many of the other large international, research-oriented agrochemical firms.   This is the story of only one of those firms, but it is typical of all of them.

Our story is divided into three main sections. Part I deals with the slow, grudging beginnings of the farm chemical business, which generally took place from 1897 to 1939. In 1939 the discovery of DDT by Paul Muller at the Ciba-Geigy firm in Basel, Switzerland, marked a sea change in the business, awakening the interest of firms and academics around the world to the potential of farm chemicals to increase food crops several fold. It also opened up the search for organic materials as insecticides and pesticides, which turned out to b e successful, and to a remarkable degree changed the complexion of agricultural chemistry almost overnight from the production of inorganic chemicals to organics. The invention of DDT changed the face of farm chemicals forever and inaugurated a new era in agriculture, an era in which the industry "grew up".10

Part II, 1939-1970, covers the era of greatest growth of the industry. In 1962 the publication of Rachel Carson's controversial magnum opus, "Silent Spring", changed things radically once again. Rachel Carson is often called "the mother of the EPA", and she probably was. When the Environmental Protection Agency came into being in 1970 as an agency of the U.S. government, replacing what had on the whole been a rather benign stewardship over farm chemicals by the U.S. Department of Agriculture with steadily more rigorous controls, the ground rules for making and selling and using farm chemicals began to be rewritten, and the period from that time hence has changed radically for farm chemicals.11

With 1970 marking the birth of the EPA, Part III is labeled "The Modern Era", 1970-2006.

We can now begin our story.

PART ONE

BEGINNINGS

1897-1939

CHRONOLOGY

PART I --
BEGINNINGS
1897-1939

1897 -- Herbert H. Dow establishes The Dow Chemical Company in Midland, Michigan, and there, behind his new house, plants his first orchard. As a hobby he begins to study the effect of the chemical products he makes on insects, fungi, and other pests of orchards and gardens.

1905 -- Dow introduces sodium benzoate as a pesticide and orchard spray but it is a failure. Instead, it becomes a leading food preservative, still used in catsup and other products today.

1907 -- The Dow company introduces its first successful agricultural chemical, liquid lime sulfur, for the control of orchard pests, the first success following 10 years of experiments in his orchards and gardens by Herbert Dow.

1912 -- Dow adds its second farm chemical, lead arsenate, which it advertises as "the most valuable insecticide known".

1918 -- Dow introduces a dry form of lime sulfur, which can either be dusted on the plant or made into a solution for spray purposes.

1919 -- Dow brings out its version of Bordeaux Mixture, most popular of the early pesticides, and calls it "Bordow". It can be applied by sprayer or duster on fruit, potatoes, vegetables, and shrubs.

1919 -- Dow begins experiments with calcium arsenate for control of the boll weevil in cotton.

1925 -- Dow hires Don Sanford, first salesman devoted exclusively to agricultural chemical sales.

1925 -- In Dow's Organic Research Laboratory, where early agricultural chemical research is centered, Drs. W. R. Veazey and E. C. Britton develop butyl pyrroline for the control of aphids. It is a great technical success but proves too toxic to humans and is never marketed.

1927 -- At the instigation of Herbert Dow, company establishes quality control in insecticide packaging.

1928 -- After tests again conducted in the orchards of H. H. Dow, Dr. Britton and Lindley E. Mills obtain a patent on a key series of insecticidal chemicals called the dinitros, opening up an important new series of insecticides to the company.

1931 -- John F. Kagy, a graduate student at Iowa State College, Ames, Iowa, develops new ways of determining a chemical's effect on insects and wins a Dow fellowship. Dow begins to send samples of chemicals for Kagy to test for insecticidal potency and there is soon a tremendous backlog. Chemicals sent to Kagy are listed as K-1, K-2, etc., which is soon called the K-List. The K-List becomes a major research tool for Dow in the ag chemical business.

1932 -- Dow's Organic Research Laboratory discovers dinitro-ortho-cyclohexylphenol, or DNOCHP, the first synthetic organic pesticide containing neither arsenic nor lead. The dinitro compounds begin to play a central role in Dow's ag chemical portfolio.

1933 -- Dow establishes a Biochemical Research Laboratory headed by Dr. Don D. Irish to investigate the potential effects of chemicals on human beings and organisms.

1934 -- Walter Dutton of the Michigan State College horticultural faculty is employed by Dow for the summers of 1934 and 1935 to work on developing a substitute for lead arsenate for codling moth control. He does this work at a property purchased by Dow at South Haven, in southwestern Michigan's fruit belt. South Haven becomes the company's first field research station for ag chemical products. Dutton becomes full-time Dow employee 1936.

1934 -- Dow establishes a Safety Department to develop, foster, and implement safe work practices.

1935 -- Methyl bromide, which Dow has been selling for use in fire extinguishers, is discovered to have insecticidal qualities and is introduced for space fumigation and for fumigation during dormancy.

1936 -- Mike sulfur is developed in response to demand for a dry wettable foliage fungicide.

1936 -- Dow hires its first medical doctor and begins a study of the symptoms caused by exposure to lead.

1937 -- A new dinitro product, Dow Spray Dormant, is introduced for dormant use on deciduous fruit trees for the control of over-wintering mites and insects.

1937 -- Facilities are set up in the Biochemical Research Laboratory to evaluate chemicals for possible ag use. Effect of chlorinated hydrocarbons and insect fumigants on mammals is studied in order to set early threshold levels for safe human exposures.

1937 -- Kagy moves to California to do research work on insecticides at the University of California Citrus Experiment Station at Riverside, inaugurating Dow's work in the citrus field.

1938 -- Iodine and Insecticides Division ("I & I") is set up at Seal Beach, California, where Dow has an iodine manufacturing plant, and Seal Beach becomes headquarters for Dow agricultural work on the West Coast. Its first ag product is "DN-Dust", first successful organic insecticide.

1938 -- Dow scientists study toxicological data on Dow products and discuss them with the Food and Drug Administration. Also this year, Dow toxicologists first test materials for their cancer-producing potential.

1939 -- Paul Muller, a Swiss citizen, synthesizes DDT, the most effective insecticide discovered to that date, and it is used by the U.S. military against malarial mosquitoes during World War II with sensational success, wiping out the disease in some parts of the world.

Herbert H. Dow

Chapter 1

Herbert H. Dow, Orchardist

He loved orchards, and it all began with his orchard. Herbert Dow was 31 years old, sporting a handlebar mustache to appear older, and had just established The Dow Chemical Company in Midland, Michigan, when he set about building a house there for his growing family. He moved into this new home two years later, in 1899, the same year in which he set out his first orchard. This consisted mainly of apple trees, but he also planted a wide variety of pears, plums, peaches, and grapes.1

He promptly began a series of experiments in his backyard Eden to determine which varieties performed best in the mid-Michigan climate. Apples were his especial delight. In the next few years he planted 85 different kinds of apple trees on his grounds and recorded their development and apple production. He carefully noted the date of planting of each tree, the date he harvested the first apple from it, the yield in pounds of each tree, and other data. Central Michigan, he soon became convinced, was destined to become the nation's leading apple area. He urged the farm boys whom he was employing in increasing numbers in his chemical plants to develop apple orchards at their farm homes. This, he pointed out, would provide them a source of healthful food as well as an added source of income.

He also began to experiment with the effects on his plantings of various of the chemicals he was making down at the plant. He would bring home some of this chemical or that and apply it to a plant or two or to a tree, and keep careful notes of the effect on the plant and its growth and yield.

In the spring of 1904 Dow bought a big four-wheeled spraying outfit for his orchard from Fairbanks, Morse, the leading manufacturer of this new-fangled piece of equipment, and began familiarizing himself with it. He taught Elzie Cote, who was becoming his gardening assistant, how to use it, too. It cost him $235, a large sum for those days, and replaced the hand sprayer he had been using, an awkward, heavy thing requiring frequent, strenuous hand pumping. An entry in his notebook indicates that he was eager to try out the newest product of his chemical factory, sodium benzoate, when he bought this new spraying rig.

A new process for making benzoate had been developed by E. O. (Ed) Barstow, a brilliant young chemist that Herbert Dow had just hired out of the Case Institute in Cleveland.   Barstow, on his way to becoming Herbert Dow's "No. 1 chemist", was running the bleach plant -- bleach was the infant Midland plant's first product -- and carrying on chemical experiments in a makeshift laboratory in a corner of the plant in his spare time. The benzoate process was his first discovery there, and made Dow the first American manufacturer of that product.

Sodium benzoate had been discovered and used as a food preservative in Germany since about the middle of the 19th century, but that was its only known use.   Herbert Dow reasoned that if it prevented the growth of fungus in food in the kitchen it would also prevent the growth of fungus in the great outdoors and therefore had to be an ideal fruit spray. 2

By July 1905 Dow and Barstow had a benzoate pilot plant in operation and were producing 100 pounds a day of the material for developmental use -- as a fruit spray, they thought.   By the end of that year he was listing it as the fourth of the company's products, following bleach, bromides, and chloroform.

Dow faced one major problem in producing benzoate, however; food additives were under intense scrutiny at the time, and the U.S. Congress, urged to do so by the U.S. Department of Agriculture, was debating whether to ban food additives entirely. This debate went on for several years and eventually resulted in passage of the Food and Drug Act in 1906 and establishment of the Food and Drug Administration to administer it. 3

Harvey W. Wiley, famous at that time as a crusader, who was then head of the USDA's Bureau of Chemistry, the forerunner of the Food and Drug Administration, had by a special act of Congress obtained authority in 1902 "to investigate the character of food preservatives, coloring matters, and other substances added to foods, to determine their relation to digestion and health, and to establish the principles which should guide their use".

This was a period when, as Wiley put it later, "All those who were preserving foods by means of chemicals were staunch in opposing legislation which would limit the trade practices they held to be legitimate and on which they supposed the life of their businesses depended. There were the manufacturers of articles used in the adulteration of foods and drugs; the so-called 'rectifiers', that is, those who made fraudulent whisky out of alcohol, colors, and flavors; the patent-medicine fraternity of fraud and hokum; the dishonest mis-branders and mis-labelers of food and drug products; and that unnumbered host engaged in business which would be controlled or eliminated entirely by a pure food law".4

Herbert Dow, on the contrary, believed sodium benzoate was simply an updated version of the smoke and salt the Indians had used from time immemorial to preserve their food, and in his view it made just as much sense to ban benzoate as it would to ban the use of smoke and salt by the Indian tribes. He shared this view frequently with the Congressmen he contacted on the subject. Even if sodium benzoate were eventually barred in food uses it would still be a big new product as an orchard spray against funguses, he reasoned, so he moved ahead with his plans for it.5

With only an embryonic sales department at his disposal (Rupert E. Paris had been hired as the company's first sales manager only a few months before, in 1904, and was now signing up customers for bleach and the other Dow products), Herbert Dow acted as the company's sales chief himself and launched his first and only product introduction campaign.

His strategy was to send sample packages of benzoate to every agricultural extension service in the U.S. and Canada, and to the leading U.S. orchards -- more than 60 in all -- asking them to try it as a spray and report back to him on the results. He invited them to ask for bigger samples if they could use them, and many did. As they knew, and as Herbert Dow knew, there was a frantic search going on nation-wide at that time for a good, reliable fungicide.

Herbert Dow had never done anything of this sort -- nation-wide sampling of a new product -- and it was a great learning experience for him and his new young company. He seems to have got the idea for this approach from a chance conversation with a fellow passenger on a New York Central train in the summer of 1905. The fellow passenger, H. J. Wheeler,

21

was director of the Rhode Island Agricultural Experiment Station at Kingston, R.I., and he described for Dow the search at his station for products to prevent mildew and fungus growths and ways to stop potato blight, and outlined their process for evaluating new agricultural products. 6

"Would you be interested in trying a fruit spray I've been working on in my orchard at home?" Dow asked him. Wheeler said he would be happy to test the material if Dow would send him a sample of it.

On his return to Midland Dow sent the sample. "Sodium benzoate is used chiefly as a preservative but it seems to prevent fungus growth when sprayed on a tree or vine as well as when canned with fruits", Dow wrote Wheeler. "Thorpe's Dictionary of Applied Chemistry (Vol. I, p. 677) states that Sodium Benzoate, one part to 2,000 parts of water, will prevent the development of bacteria as well as Copper Sulphate, at one part to 133 parts of water. It would be interesting to know if this same superiority exists in preventing fungus growths. If so, it would be much cheaper than Copper Sulphate as it is probably 15 times as effective and only costs about five times as much".

"The use of Sodium Benzoate as a fungicidal spray is new; at least we know of no such work having previously been done", Dow wrote. "Being a matter of great general interest and importance, it is hoped that you will make a place for it among your other tests, and we shall be glad to send you a further supply should you desire it".7

Another to whom Herbert Dow wrote was the renowned Luther Burbank, the wizard who was developing new plant varieties out in California, whom he had visited. He wrote Burbank that he had experimented "as follows -- to 50 gals. of weak Bordeaux was added four ounces of Sodium Benzoate. Insoluble Copper Benzoate was formed, which caused the mixture to adhere more firmly to the foliage than does the ordinary Bordeaux. The fungicidal effect appeared", he wrote, "to be markedly increased, but systematic and extended trials not having as yet been made this conclusion cannot, of course, be absolutely depended upon".8

Another of Dow's famous correspondents on the subject was George Washington Carver of the Tuskegee Institute in Alabama, of which

Booker T. Washington was then the principal. Carver, the black genius who developed peanut butter and other food products in his Tuskegee laboratory, told Dow his first package of benzoate had arrived at Tuskegee "too late in the season for spraying experiments", but expressed interest in trying it, which he did in the following season. In 1907 Dow wrote him to ask if he had any results to report. Carver replied that he had used the material "for another experimental field in which I am working, and that is preserving of fruits for exhibition purposes. I found it works admirably so far, much better than I had any idea, and I shall perform more experiments in that direction as I am putting up quite a large collection for exhibitive purposes".9

In the meanwhile the "battle of benzoate" was heating up in Washington as Wiley pressed his crusade. Herbert Dow was startled by a news item of July 14, 1908 reporting that the U.S. government "May Bar Benzoate of Soda". "It is likely that a ban will be placed on benzoate of soda, which is largely used by manufacturers as a food preservative, as a result of investigations made by Prof. John Long of the Northwestern University of Chicago", it was reported. "Dr. Long is one of the men appointed by the president (then Theodore Roosevelt) to act as referee in disputes between the bureau of chemistry of the Department of Agriculture and the manufacturers of the country. The Chicago experiments confirm the position taken by Dr. Wiley and other scientific men in Washington. The manufacturers fought the decisions of the bureau of chemistry and took their grievances to the president, who appointed the board of five scientists to review the disputed points".10

Dow wrote Harvey Hackenberg of the Dow board of directors in Cleveland that he was surprised such a report should come out so soon. "Usually", he commented drily, "experts who are employed by the United States Government are not looking for an opportunity to cut down the time of their employment."

"We hope", he added, "within a year or two to be unaffected by any action that the Government may take regarding food preservatives, as we think the sale of Benzoate as a fungicide will prove to be a more profitable field".11

He turned out to be wrong about this. Sales of Sodium Benzoate were rapidly declining as a result of the Wiley campaign. And as a spray it had a major flaw -- it protected the fruit tree only until the first rain shower had washed it away. Herbert Dow tried Calcium Benzoate, which was less soluble, as a replacement. It took another couple of years of experiments to show that the calcium variety was more persistent, but not as effective as a fungicide.

As a food preservative, however, the Dow company sold sodium benzoate for many years. Dr. Wiley and the U.S. goverment put strict limits on its use in foods but it is still used today, a century later, in catsup and other products, as a preservative.

It was always hard for Herbert Dow to give up on a project or an idea but occasionally he was obliged to do so, and this was one of those cases. The sodium benzoate venture, as it turned out, became a crucial learning experience for his entree, and that of his company, into the field of agricultural chemicals although it was in itself a failure.

Within a few years he was embarked on new explorations in the agricultural chemical field as he and his company began to take a broader vision of the possibilities of providing chemical weapons for the farmer and orchardist and gardener against their six-legged enemies the insects and the fungi and their relatives.

In 1907 he began to produce the first successful farm product of the company, liquid lime sulfur, which was effective against a variety of orchard pests, and the birth of farm chemicals in the company is usually dated from the quiet, unheralded introduction of this product. Made by boiling together lime, sulfur, and water, liquid lime sulfur is still used today as a fungicidal spray on fruit trees.

Five years later the company began to make and sell lead arsenate, its first true insecticide. The sulfurics and the arsenicals became the main pesticides of the next generation.

Both of these compounds -- liquid lime sulfur and lead arsenate -- were developed in trials made in Herbert Dow's orchard, a practice that continued until his death in 1930. A major breakthrough came in 1928, when Dr. E. C. Britton and a fellow researcher, Lindley E. Mills, discovered a new family of insecticides, the "dinitros", which they patented after another series of trials in the Dow orchards. The dinitros were to be key pesticides and a major force in the market until World War II, and for many years afterward.

Herbert Dow's journals indicate that he continued to experiment with various chemicals in his gardens and orchards all his life. Here are a few entries from his Garden Book No. 3, covering the period from 1918 to 1930, into which he sometimes mixed in notes about what was going on down at the plant or in the family::

June 29, 1918 -- "Delicious (a variety of apple tree) N (north) of grape vines on higher ground is beginning to look dry. Will let hose run on it all night and will note effect on fruit buds for next year. Everything very dry. Pond two inches below overflow. Two single dahlias B to B (beginning to bloom), many budded. Sprayed S (south) row twice in Teal orchard, next row once, third row once, with magnesium bisulfite, 3 lbs to 50 gal. Sprayed peach 4 times in 1 1/4 hrs. Also sprayed cherries and Japan plums nearest barn". (Note added later -- "Later results showed burning on peaches only").

August 11, 1922 -- "Hail storm. Some stones 2" diameter, some 3" long. All fruit severely damaged. 2 panes of glass in barn broken, 1 broken and 2 cracked in greenhouse. All fruit should be sprayed with Ca salicylate".

August 7, 1924 -- "Kettering & Midgley here. Talk of using 600,000 lbs. Bromine per month". ("Boss" Kettering of General Motors and Thomas Midgeley, inventors of Ethyl gas, were looking for a reliable source of bromine for the production of Ethyl gas. Dow became that source)12

August 30, 1925 -- "Sunday. Irrigated Teal orchard again using a pail full of sodium nitrate, potassium nitrate, ammonium sulfate and phosphate. Cold weather of two nights previous has apparently colored apples very much. Weather has been dry recently but the effect of the 4" rainfall the first week in August is shown in the large size of apples for the season and the heavy dews, Size however is most apparent in Teal orchard where the rainfall was preceded on July 19 by an irrigation using potassium and sodium nitrates..

September 13, 1925 -- "Used mixed sodium nitrate, potassium nitrate & acid phosphate and ammonium sulfate on Cortland (another variety of apple) in Teal orchard, also on Delicious near cinder curves near top of hill near Lombardy poplars. This Cortland has been nitrated at least 3 times since spring but the apples are no larger than those on .... trees at end of Spy row". 13

In 1920 Herbert Dow was a key figure in the formatiion of the first Rotary Club in Midland, and when he came to fill out an application form for membership he was asked to specify his profession. "Orchardist", he wrote.

It seems to have been there that he felt most at home.

.

William Hale

Chapter 2

Billy Hale and the Carbon Club

As was customary in the small-town, small-company America of the early
20th century, Herbert Dow hired many of his own relatives to work in his
growing chemical enterprise. He hired his own sons, his sons-in-law, his
brother-in-law. Even his own father was for a time on the company
payroll. So was his wife, Grace, who was briefly a member of its board of
directors.

The practice caused him no end of grief. Tom Griswold, who had married
Herbert Dow's younger sister, for example, was a highly capable engineer
and one of the first people he hired, but while Tom made many worthy
contributions to the company he also had a habit of wandering about the
plant and giving "suggestions" to the workforce that they felt obliged to
adopt, not knowing whether Tom was carrying a message for Herbert Dow
or speaking for himself, and afraid to find out.

By far the worst of his problems in this respect, however, was the young
man who married Helen, his eldest daughter. His name was William J.
Hale, professor of chemistry, a specialist in organic chemistry at the
University of Michigan. Helen followed her brother Willard to Ann Arbor
for a college education and enrolled in some chemistry classes, as
recommended by her father and brother. There she met Willard's good
friend Prof. Hale, a handsome, smartly-dressed young swain then known
as the "Beau Brummel" of the campus, and the two fell in love and in
February, 1917, were married. Prof. Hale was 41, his student bride was
23. 1

In February, 1918, she gave birth to a girl they named Ruth. Disaster
struck the happy couple a few months later, in October, when Helen was
carried off by the great flu pandemic of 1918. She was ill only a few
days, and then suddenly died, a typical pattern for that strain of influenza.
The young husband and father was shattered. He dropped his teaching
duties on the spot, and told the university he was unable to continue his
work.

In his grief he turned to his father-in-law for help, asking what he should do. In short order Hale's widowed mother, Emma Elizabeth Hale, arrived from Dayton, Ohio, and took the baby in hand, an arrangement that soon became permanent. Hale said he didn't think he could or wanted to go back to teaching at Ann Arbor. His father-in-law asked if he'd like to go to work for The Dow Chemical Company. "I hadn't thought of that", Hale said.

But without very much more conversation and after thinking about it, Hale became director of Organic Chemical Research for the Dow company and moved to Midland. Herbert Dow and Billy Hale set to work mapping out a program of organic chemical research for the Dow company.

As the two men discussed their plans Dow began to realize that he didn't really know very much about organic chemistry. Up to then his focus had been on inorganic chemistry, and he was extremely successful at it. But he had done hardly anything at all in organic chemistry. Could Billy Hale, he asked, give him and others in the company a refresher course, an update, in the rudiments of organic chemistry? Prof. Hale said he would be delighted to do that.

Their conversations resulted in the formation of what they called "the Carbon Club" (organic compounds contain a carbon atom), which met once a week in the Education Building, next door to company headquarters, for 10 weeks. Here Herbert Dow and about 30 of the senior managers of the company learned, or relearned, the basics of organic chemistry from Prof. Hale. Another lecture series of a more advanced nature followed during the summer of 1919.2

They called it the "Carbon Club" to conceal to some degree the fact that the senior managers of the firm were going back to school, and no publicity outside the company was given the matter.

As a result, at the end of World War I, during which time these activities were going on, the Dow company was fully prepared to enter, and did enter, the organic chemical world, and as it turned out, Billy Hale was absolutely right -- organic chemistry would be the dominant field in the world's chemical industry for the next century or two.

The arrival of Prof. William J. Hale in the affairs of the Dow company, and his introduction of organic chemistry to the company, was nothing short of a miraculous event, a major turning point in the company's history. Without him the Dow company could very well have continued to work the inorganic side of the chemical street indefinitely, and have continued to prosper as a small, successful firm. But coming to the company as he did, at precisely the right time, was something of a heaven-sent accident.

Billy Hale had more influence on the future of the company than anyone at that time realized, and it can persuasively be argued that it was he who put the company on the path to becoming the world's largest chemical company. The firms that continued to mine the inorganic lode exclusively, over time, became only secondary factors in the chemical industry. He turned out to be the right person, at the right time, in the right circumstances, to land on Herbert Dow's doorstep.

It is sad and ironic that Herbert Dow had to give up his first-born child for this to happen.

William Jay Hale was born in Ada, Ohio, on January 5, 1876, and was called "Billy" almost from the beginning. His father, the Rev. James T. Hale, a Presbyterian minister, moved periodically from one Ohio congregation to another throughout Billy's youth. The young man was a brilliant student and developed an affinity for chemistry at an early age. (His father thought he should become either a minister or a professor of Greek). He earned A.B. and M.A. degrees from Miami University of Ohio, and then went on to Harvard, where he earned an A.B. in 1898, an M.A. in 1899, and a Ph.D. in 1902. To complete his schooling he spent a year as a traveling fellow in chemistry at the Technische Hochschule in Berlin and at the University of Goettingen, in Germany, then generally considered to be among the top chemical schools in the world. During his time in Europe he developed an unbounded admiration for everything German, a sentiment he did nothing to conceal back in the United States during two World Wars, causing all kinds of problems for himself and his family and others with whom he was associated, including most conspicuously the Dow company.   He was as a result often accused of being pro-German, which he was, and pro-Nazi, which he was not

He taught chemistry at the University of Chicago for a term in 1903 and then came to the University of Michigan, where he was an instructor in chemistry until 1908, an assistant professor until 1915, and an associate professor from 1915 until the time he left. During his years at Ann Arbor he published three chemistry textbooks and 23 research papers.

During his time at Dow he felt free to walk unannounced into any office or lab or meeting room and participate in whatever was going on. If the subject didn't interest him, or bored him, he would get up and walk out. Between that and his pro-German stance, Willard Dow, then president of Dow (and Billy's brother-in-law), finally had to ask Hale to use his own stationery for his correspondence, not the Dow company's.3

A typical story of Billy Hale was that Clarence Macomber, president of the largest bank in Midland, once stopped Herbert Dow on Main Street and asked him, "Say, what's the matter with that son-in-law of yours, Dr. Hale? We keep sending him OD notices but he keeps right on writing checks". Dow said he'd look into it, and when he saw Hale asked him about it. "OD means 'Over Drawn'?" Billy exclaimed, bursting into laughter. "I thought it meant 'On Deposit'. I thought someone was putting money into my account that I didn't know about, so every time I got an OD notice I went out and spent it". 4

It was commonly said of Billy that he was too much ahead of his time. Much of his early research activity was devoted to chlorophyll, which he was convinced was "good for you", and he was concerned years before anyone else was that cigarettes and tobacco were not "good for you". He therefore developed a cigarette containing chlorophyll that he called the "Hale" -- his slogan for them was "Inhale with Hale" -- fashioned of light green paper with a chlorophyll filter tip. They didn't sell very well, and eventually disappeared. "They literally went up in smoke", he said, smiling in his roguish way.

His most successful venture in this field was a chlorophyll cigar, called the "Crest" cigar, made by a company in Richmond, Virginia. "After he died

I would still get a check for something like $15 once in a while, for the Crest cigar", his daughter, Ruth Hale Buchanan, said.

He tried to introduce chlorophyll into the American diet in every way he could think of -- chlorophyll chocolate bars, chlorophyll toothpaste, chlorophyll coffee, chlorophyll chewing gum, all of which he patented. He set up a company to provide chlorophyll in proper forms for these ventures and others, the Verdurin Company of Detroit and Midland, Michigan, of which he was of course president.5

The chlorophyll gum venture was fairly typical of his inventions, most of which he tried to manufacture and sell himself, or at least keep under his control. At first he called it "Vita-Green Gum", and later he called it "Phyllets" and marketed it in a small green and orange box. "He was bound and determined that everybody should chew Phyllets", his daughter Ruth said. "Chlorophyll was good for you, and would make your breath fresh. He didn't advertise; he put it in a drug store down on K Street and Connecticut Avenue (in Washington, D.C.) I will never forget; he had me and Wiley (Wiley T. Buchanan, her husband, who some years later became President Eisenhower's Chief of Protocol) one day, standing there on the corner handing out these damn Phyllets to anybody that came by. He said, 'Just pass them out'. We did it. After that he said, 'Oh no, I just can't be bothered advertising. This man Mr. Wolf has offered to buy me out'. So Mr. Wolf bought him out and those are now Clorets. He would have made a fortune on Clorets had he stuck with the Phyllets, but he didn't. He never worried about anything like that. Mr. Wolf began to advertise, and it was everywhere; later you still saw it on television; you see chlorophyll advertised everywhere. But my father never believed in advertising. If the thing sold itself, it sold; if it didn't, you just couldn't worry about that. He could invent it, but in the sales department he was awful, terrible. He just didn't know about it."6

Billy sold his patent on chlorophyll chewing gum for $100, she said. It is still marketed worldwide today as Clorets.

His most important invention for Dow Chemical was a new method, the chlorobenzene process, for the manufacture of phenol, later hailed as one of the 10 most important patents in Dow company history. As a result of this invention, Dow became for many years the world's largest producer of this key chemical. His partner in this invention was Edgar C. Britton, who had been his assistant at Ann Arbor, and who became his assistant at the Dow Organic Research Laboratory in Midland in 1925.7

"Doc" Britton took over the Organic Research Laboratory when Hale left in 1932 and developed many of the products that fed Dow's growth. He is credited with 354 patents, more than any other individual in Dow history, and the laboratory he and Billy Hale established has been called the Britton Laboratory in his honor since 1953.

Hale is remembered chiefly today, however, as the father of chemurgy, which Webster's defines as that "branch of applied chemistry that deals with industrial utilization of organic raw materials, especially from farm products". Perhaps the most common example is the use of corn to produce ethanol as a component of gasoline; E-85, sold at such stations, consists of 15 per cent gasoline and 85 per cent ethanol. The chemurgic movement advocated the use of the expanding farm surpluses of the 1920's for industrial purposes such as gasohol rather than plowing them under, as was then a growing practice.8

In 1919 Hale purchased an old farm near West Branch, Michigan, northeast of Midland. He grew ruffed grouse there, and every fall invited some of his chemist friends there for "pat hunting". In 1925 he and Charles H. Herty, a leading authority on cellulose chemistry (president of the American Chemical Society, 1915-16) sat down on a log at the farm and had a conversation that lasted several hours about the farm problems in the United States and what to do about them.

Herty, based on this conversation, wrote a series of articles on the farm surplus problem for scientific journals, and Hale, who was a popular after-dinner speaker, began pushing the idea of gasohol in his speeches, and wrote a long article titled, "Farming Must Become a Chemical Industry: Development of Co-Products Will Solve the Present Agricultural Crisis", but which no one was willing to print. One day Hale received a telegram from William J. Cameron, editor of the Dearborn (MI) Independent, a newspaper owned by Henry Ford, asking "May we publish this immediately?" He gave permission, and it was printed there in October, 1926.9 It was a big hit. Cameron's office was overwhelmed with requests for reprints of it, and he published it in leaflet form. Still the requests kept coming in, and eventually Hale's friends at the Chemical Foundation in New York took over the task and quickly exhausted a press run of 500,000 copies. "That was the beginning of the chemurgic movement", Herty said, the first delineation of the idea of chemurgy.

The first actual use of the word "chemurgy", coined by Hale as a companion term to metallurgy, occurred in a book Hale published in 1934, "The Farm Chemurgic: Farmward the Star of Destiny Lights Our Way". 10

In 1935 Hale's friend Francis P. Garvan, president of the Chemical Foundation, convened what they called the "First Joint Conference of Agriculture, Industry, and Science" in Dearborn, Michigan, under the auspices of Henry Ford and the Ford Motor Company, to organize the movement in a more formal way. Ford himself, famous for his experiments in making automobile parts from soybeans and golden rod, made brief appearances at the meetings. Garvan was elected first president of the National Farm Chemurgic Council, which then became the governing board of the movement. The Council met annually until World War II, with Hale playing the role of senior statesman. Hale, Herty, and Garvan are generally considered the founders of the movement, which periodically becomes lively again -- especially in times of oil crisis, when alternatives to crude oil become more attractive and interesting.11

Garvan died in 1937 and Herty in 1938, and the chemurgic movement began to lose its steam after that. Hale penned a full half-dozen books over the years heartily supportive of the movement -- "Chemistry Triumphant", in 1932, "The Farm Chemurgic", 1934, "Prosperity Beckons", 1936, "Farmward March", 1939, "Farmer Victorious", 1949, and "Chemivision", 1952.

His contributions were enormous, but are largely forgotten today. He established the American Chemical Society chapter in Midland. He founded the Dow Chemical Library, starting with a grant of $10,000 from the Dow board of directors with which to buy books. It is now one of the world's premier chemical libraries. He ramrodded, as chairman of its editorial committee, what is still today the only full-length history of the U.S. chemical industry, written by his friend Williams Haynes between the years 1938 and 1954, and finally published in six volumes in 1954.12

Most of all, though, he brought the viewpoint of sophisticated European chemistry, then dominant in the chemical world, to a small backwoods chemical company in Michigan, and pointed the way to its future.

Ethanol production in the U.S. rose from 2.14 billion gallons in 2002 to almost six billion gallons in 2006. The production of the corn to produce that ethanol climbed from 996 million bushels in 2002 to 2.2 billion bushels in 2006 13 Billy Hale's predictions of many years before were coming true.

"He was just a half-an-hour before his time", his grand-daughter Bonnie Buchanan Matheson said. "He missed it. I liked him, but he was argumentative. I was told that he was argumentative and that he would argue the opposite point of almost anything, just to get the thing going, to get people thinking. I thought that was kind of cool, even though it was told to me as a criticism of him. There were certain things that he said over and over. 'Don't eat salt, it's bad for you. American Indians don't eat salt'. 'Coffee is poisonous. Don't drink coffee'. And sugar -- 'Don't eat sugar. It's terrible for you'. Of course, if you saw his picture, he ate sugar. I don't think he drank coffee actually, but he ate sugar and he loved candy and good food and rich food. I can remember him saying to Mother, 'Don't let these children have candy'. I thought, 'I don't like that. We'll have to keep him away'. But he was cheerful and he would talk about world peace, and that there would be another war, 'the third World War', he would say, 'and then after that there would be a thousand years of peace'. I kept thinking, 'Gosh, I want to get through that so we can get to the thousand years of peace'.14

Don Sanford

Chapter 3

The Night Wrangler

One day in 1925 a young man wearing cowboy boots and a stetson came
into the crowded, scruffy headquarters of the Dow Chemical Company in
Midland, Michigan, and asked to talk to someone in the sales department.
The arrival of a cowboy was a highly unusual event in Midland in 1925
and he was soon escorted in to talk to Lee Doan, the assistant sales
manager.

The young man said his name was Don Sanford and that he had learned
quite a bit about selling agricultural chemicals to farmers and ranchers and
orchard people in his travels and he wondered if the company had any
openings for someone in that field. "We don't have an Agricultural
Chemicals department", Doan said. "Why don't we start one?" Sanford
asked. "Why don't I start it?"1

They talked a few minutes and Doan rapidly began to like the idea of a
specialist selling ag chemicals. "I'm inclined to hire you," he told
Sanford, "but I can't do it without a little authority". He went out into a
little hallway and came back in a few minutes and said, "Well, I'm going
to hire you". "Who decided for you?" Sanford asked. Doan said, "I went
to see my boss, Mr. Bennett". "Who's he?" Sanford asked. "He's the
fellow who handles the money around here", Doan said, "and I met a
friend of yours when I was in his office".

"That's surprising", Sanford said, "I don't know anyone around here".
"Yes, you do", Doan said. "Our legal department was in there talking to
Mr. Bennett". "How would I know your legal department?", Sanford
asked. "We just have one lawyer, and that's Mr. Gilbert Currie", Doan
told him. "Mr. Currie listened to us, and I told them there was a fellow
named Don Sanford here". Currie asked, "Does he come from out in the
country here, down Freeland way?". Doan said "Yes, he does". Currie
said, "Hire him. I know his people."2

So it was that Don Sanford was hired as Dow's first agricultural chemicals
salesman, almost 30 years before the company established a formal
agricultural chemicals department. "My territory (to start with) was all

the United States and all of Canada, and about half of Mexico", Sanford said, "and I didn't really have any supervisor. I knew where the business was and how to get it, so I went out and got it".

Sanford was literally "turned loose" to show how he could sell agricultural chemicals and was quickly a success. "I'm a traveling man", Sanford said. "Always was. I went anywhere I thought I could get some business. I knew what they grew, and I knew what kind of materials they needed, and when they were going to need them, and I took it from there".

He covered his vast territory by train and automobile. "There was no flying in those days", he said. "Sometimes I drove a company car and sometimes I drove mine and they gave me mileage. I drove about 50,000 miles a year. I traded cars about twice a year. I used mostly Fords. I drove Chryslers and Buicks, Fords. Never drove Chevrolets. It was running good all the time, hardly ever had to change a tire. Chrysler was the finest, quietest, nicest car I ever drove, but through my driving time, before I started flying, I had 17 Ford convertibles, and I loved them. My last car I drove before I got my shoulder busted up and had to quit, was a little Ford Ranch Wagon. I hauled hay, barb wire, fence posts, little colts and everything in the world. I liked Fords".

His traveling switched to airplanes around 1945, at the end of World War II. "Earlier than that there wasn't any way to fly", he said. "Then, when other folks started flying, it got to where I had to, to keep up. I did a lot of flying".

On occasion Sanford even did his selling on horseback. "Quite a few places, like in Ohio", he said, "it is real hilly down in southern Ohio, and this clay....I had an old boy named Jim Stockline had a nice orchard way up on top of one of these hills -- there was a road up to the orchard, but in the spring in wet weather when I was there the only way to get up there was to ride a horse. I did it a lot of places. That southern Ohio country -- there's a county down there, Lawrence County, close to the river, and quite a lot of orchards in there. Well, when the weather was clear and the roads dried up, all the competition began coming in, I would ride a horse up in there and I'd have my business all tied up before they ever got around toget there".

When he started out in 1925 Dow didn't have have very much in the way of farm chemicals for him to sell. "We had an insecticide, arsenate of lead", he said. "We had two types, what we called the wet and the dry. We had a paste lead and a powdered lead, and that was a spray for apples, codling moth and other insects, and for a fungicide we had a liquid lime sulfur, and a dry lime sulfur, and that was for scab, scale and that sort of thing, and then we had a copper product that was a good fungicide called Dowco.

"We really didn't have much of a line, but gradually we began expanding it", he said. "Old Doc Veazey had quite a lot of agricultural experiments going on for quite a long time, and he believed in me, and in Ag Chemicals, and any time we needed a little help, he would get it for us."3

He sold mainly to jobbers and dealers. "Until I could find a good jobber I'd sell to dealers direct", he said. "Occasionally I sold to a big grower, if it made sense. We didn't tie it up so tight that you couldn't deviate from it. I was given the privilege to sell the way I wanted to".

"For several years I pretty much did the selling (in the agricultural chemicals area)", he said. "It worked all right. Then we began to get some products that the company would kind of like to try out under our own label and some of those things, like weed killers and the like, and that changed things pretty fast. I always told them I'd love to be in the small package Dow-label business, as long as I didn't have anything to do with it. I didn't like it and still don't. I liked to sell carloads, not nickel and dime stuff. I wasn't much interested in selling a case or two".

Within a few years he was one of the star salesmen of the company. "One year", he said, "I can't be quite certain of the date, but it would have been about 1927 or 1928, we, in my corner in Ag Chemicals, we sold everything due to go to July and shipped it out in June, and we had a million-dollar month in my department. And that year, it was either '27 or '28, sales for the entire Dow Chemical Company were $12 million dollars".

Sanford had started out his career as a real-life cowboy. He came from a place called Red Lodge, Montana, in the Beartooth Mountains not far from the Wyoming state line and about 25 miles from Yellowstone

National Park. "That was her home too", he said, referring to his late wife. "I have had relatives all over Montana. We (he and his wife) kind of grew up there. I had four uncles that ranched out of Billings, and I have an aunt that ranched up in Libby, Montana, and I had most of my bringing up in Montana." That is prime cowboy country, and he grew up as one, spending much of every day on horseback. In 1916, when he was 20, he enlisted in the U.S. cavalry, which during World War I was still an important component of the U.S. Army. The U. S. had not yet entered the war.

In the cavalry, he was night wrangler for a herd of brood mares. "We were still raising horses for the cavalry", he said. "The Army was looking for good horses. There were 34 brood mares in that herd. I was the night wrangler there for about six months. It was quite a job. They'd do their grazing in the daytime, and your job was to keep them calmed down and quieted at night. It didn't always work that way. Get a good thunderstorm and they'd come apart on you. It paid pretty good money -- $30 a month."

In March of 1916 the Mexican general Pancho Villa made an abortive and unwise raid on the border town of Columbus, New Mexico, in which 18 Americans died, and hustled back into Mexico. General John J. ("Black Jack") Pershing was dispatched by the U.S. government on what was called a "Punitive Expedition" into Mexico, looking for :Pancho Villa, and Sanford and the 13th Cavalry went with him.

"It wasn't very bad", Sanford said. "Eight or 10 of our men were killed, I guess. I was in the 13th Cavalry, in L Troop, then. Pancho Villa headed back into Mexico, and we took after him, and we could have gotten him any time we wanted him -- we knew where he was, but we didn't want to get him. It was what was called a punitive expedition, just out to punish him a little bit".

As it turned out, chasing Pancho Villa was just a warm-up for action in the big world war that was going on over in Europe. "We came right out of Mexico and went directly to France", Sanford said. "And that was all a part of the deal in the beginning -- they didn't need to chase him, and didn't want to get him, but it was a good way to get a lot of experience and if you didn't have something going on you couldn't get the enlistments you needed, so that was all part of getting ready for the first World War".

"We had kind of rough going for awhile in France", Sanford said. "I came out pretty lucky, though. Lost a lot of horses and mules". It was the last world conflict in which the horse cavalry played a role.

"When we finished the first World War and the Army of Occupation got ready, I spent a lot of time taking horses up into the Army of Occupation. We just nicely got them up there and located and ready to serve the Army of Occupation when the government came out with these little crawl tractors, and we went up and brought the horses back out and put the tractors in. Then I spent about six or eight more months selling mules and horses. We had ten or twelve thousand that it didn't pay to bring back -- it would cost more to bring them back than they were worth. So we sold a good many thousands of them. We did it by auction sales, all over France.

"The French had mules down in southern France and in the Pyrenees mountains, they used mules down there, but these big mules of ours from Arkansas and Tennessee, they just didn't understand them. In fact, once in awhile we'd sell a mule to a Frenchman, tonight he'd take him home, and tomorrow morning he'd be back wanting to give him back to us".

By the time he mustered out of the cavalry his father had settled down on a spread on the Tittabawassee river at Smiths Crossing, not far from Midland and the Dow company.

.

Earl Bennett, who had been instrumental in hiring him, became one of his heroes. "He was a grand man, Mr. Bennett was", he said. "He was small in stature but one of the biggest in heart, temperament and ability and understanding. We had lots of times when credit was a problem, and our entire Credit Department at that time was Mr. Lew A. Chichester. He rode with me quite a lot of times. I tried to keep my accounts responsible but I went through a couple of depressions in Dow, and they were a little rough, but Bennett would take a chance. Let's say a fellow might have quite a deal on peaches maybe down in Georgia and it could be a grape thing over in Pennsylvania -- there were some good grape vineyards over there -- and I had a company could distribute for us pretty good, they weren't a highly capitalized company, but they ran a good sound show, and I said to Mr. Bennett, 'What would you do if I brought in quite a lot of orders here for quite a lot of money from these people, on credit, and this was just the first order, there could be more later", and he said, 'I'll tell you what let's do. Sell them this first order, give it to them on credit, and let them understand it's up to them to get it sold and get their money for it'. That makes a lot of sense, and that's the way he ran that department."

Sanford said that when Hetty Green, the famous "witch of Wall Street", died, it posed a major problem for Bennett. She had acquired a large amount of Dow Chemical stock early in her career and it had skyrocketed in value. "This stock was going to go on the market, and Dow wasn't really very big, and it was a little too much to dump on the market all at once, it would affect the price. Mr. Bennett financed the deal and took the whole thing", he said. "He didn't put it on the market, he sold it to us on credit, pay as you earned it. Quite a lot of the stock I had started with that deal."

"I always had fun in this sales deal", Sanford said. "It was and is a good kind of business. I had good products, and if I would go into an area and do a good job I always left it a little better than I found it. A fellow growing peaches, apples or grapes, after I had a good workout with him, he could do a better job than he had done before. And then came the weedkillers and that was fun. That was 2,4-D. I had big business up in Canada out of Calgary in the big wheat provinces, taking out ragweed, mustard. You got such a wonderful improvement with it, you know. It did such a good job. You could have a field of wheat and it would be just yellow with mustard. You'd go in there and you'd do the job right, in about four days you couldn't see a single mustard plant and it never hurt the wheat a bit. It didn't hurt the narrow-leaf product but the wide ones, like mustard. You did such a good job, it was fun to see what you had done".

He retired when he was 65, in August 1961, as the rules required, but didn't stop being a traveling man. Nor did he discontinue his lifelong love of horses. When he was 86 years old he was training a horse one day, as he still loved to do. In this exercise the horse circled around him on a long tether in a circular corral as he taught it to start and stop with voice commands. Sanford fainted during this process with no advance warning, and as he lay on the ground unconscious but still holding the tether, the horse kept right on circling around him, literally twisting his arm almost off as he did so. He recovered his health but lost the use of his right arm

44

completely, and went to live in a convalescent/retirement home at Brighton, Colorado, where his son lived.

He will be remembered as one of the most colorful, tireless, and enthusiastic of the bug fighters, one who enjoyed every moment of a pioneering career.

PART TWO

GROWING UP

1939 - 1970

PART TWO --
GROWING UP
1939-1970

1939 -- Dow introduces chloropicrin as a soil fumigant.

1940 -- Dow Selective Weed Killer, another dinitrophenol herbicide, is introduced.

1941 -- On August 1, Dow establishes its first laboratory devoted specifically to study of agricultural problems, including greenhouses and field research areas, at Seal Beach, with Kagy as lab director.

1941 -- Dow initiates first metabolism studies of fumigants on animals, and begins to investigate effect of chronic exposures to lead arsenate and other lead compounds.

1942 -- A veterinary research unit is established by Dow in Midland under Dr. Julius E. Johnson to study animal disease control and nutrition, with initial emphasis on poultry coccidiosis, the most common disease of poultry, and the use of methionine as a feed supplement. Its mission is soon broadened to cover a wide range of animal parasites and nutritional problems.

1943 -- Dow begins research in soil fumigation at Seal Beach, the main initial target being the sugar-beet wireworm, working closely with M. W. Stone of the USDA Laboratories at Whittier and Oxnard, California. The first fumigant resulting is ethylene dibromide, patented by Kagy and Robert R. McPherson. The product is called Dowfume W-40, later improved by William R. Hanson and called Dowfume W-10.

1945 -- Dow begins manufacture of DDT in formulations ranging from a 3% dust to a 20% emulsifiable spray.

1945 -- First issue of "Down to Earth", A Review of Agricultural Chemical Progress, is mailed by Dow to 13,000 workers in agricultural research in the U.S. and Canada. Dow pledges the journal will publish news of general interest to the field "whether or not Dow is a principal producer of the product involved". Editor is Eugene E. Perrin.

1945 -- Premerge, an improved dinitro product, is introduced for weed control in peas. The product is later used for weed and grass control in small seeded legumes, potatoes, beans, corn, peanuts, and other crops, such as gladiolus.

1946 -- Dow replaces its First Aid Dept. with a full-scale Medical Department.

1948 -- Harold R. Hoyle, Dow's first full-time industrial hygienist, is hired to study the effect of exposing humans to chemicals under working conditions. In this year the company also begins continuous monitoring of air pollutants in a production plant by use of instrumentation, monitoring carbon tet vapors in its aspirin plant, probably the first continuous monitoring instrumentation employed anywhere.

1949 -- Additional field station established at Sacramento, California.

1949 -- A new, odorized methyl bromide is introduced under the name Dowfume MC-2

1950 -- Production of methionine begins in a new plant at Pittsburg, California. One of the basic amino acids, methionine has been synthesized by Dr. Britton and is marketed as a feed additive for dairy animals.

1951 -- Dow develops a promising new herbicide and calls it Dalapon.

1951 -- Dow studies persistence of pesticides in soil and persistence of herbicides in water, and conducts plant residue studies. It also initiates fish toxicity studies involving effluent and pesticides.

1952 -- An Agricultural Chemicals Department is established as a separate division of the Dow company, with Joseph W. (Bill) Britton as general manager, W. W. (Bill) Allen as sales manager, Julius E. Johnson as research director, and Keith C. Barrons as manager of field research and development.

1952 -- Dow establishes research laboratory specializing in veterinary and feed chemical work at Freeport, Texas.

1953 -- Dow begins research in the chloropyridines in its West Coast laboratories.

1953 -- Research station for cotton research is opened by Dow at Greenville, Mississippi.

1953 -- Agricultural Chemical Development becomes a separate section of the Agricultural Chemicals Department of Dow.

1954 -- Three new selective weed killers are introduced to the market -- Magron, Kuron, and Dalapon -- as well as a new miticide called Ovotran, for use in citrus and other fruit crops.

1957 -- Dow purchases 200-acre tract on outskirts of Midland for agricultural field test work and closes the South Haven Field Station.

1960 -- Dow introduces Zoalene, a new coccidiostat, also called Zoamix.

1960 -- Company conducts its first pesticide residue study on fish..

1960 -- New agricultural research center at Midland begins full-scale operation. Research facilities at Seal Beach are improved and enlarged.

1961 -- Dow Crabgrass Killer is introduced and is an immediate hit. By 1962 it is the leading product in its field.

1962 -- Ag research field station is opened at Davis, California, and a poultry research facility at Fayetteville, Arkansas.

1962 -- In a reorganization move, Dow sets up a Bioproducts Department which includes pharmaceuticals, biologicals, animal health, and agricultural products.

1962 -- Dow introduces N-Serve, a new product which prolongs nitrogen fertilizer applications, and Ruelene, a new animal health product for control of cattle grubs and of internal parasites in sheep. Also launched is a new line of lawn and garden products with the Dowpon Grass Killer Bar and Novege, an all-purpose weed killer.

1963 -- New product introductions continue with Tordon herbicide, especially effective in controlling brush and perennial weeds, and Sirlene, a feed and water supplement for farm stock and pets.

1964 -- New general anesthetic for veterinary use, trademarked Metafane, is introduced along with a new Daxtron herbicide and a promising new insecticide, Dursban.

1964 -- Company studies effects on the cholinesterase levels in rats of vapors from insecticide-treated surfaces, simulating house treatments, and carries out the first fish and Daphnia reproduction tests and the first bioconcentration tests on fish and Daphnia with picloram.

1965 -- Production facilities are expanded for 2,4-D, 2,4,5-T, Sodium TCA, methyl bromide, Tordon, and Norbak, a particulating agent which controls drift from sprays.

1966 -- Dursban undergoes pre-registration testing for use against mosquitoes and is already being used for chinch bug control in Florida and tick control in Australia. Sales of a new Coyden coccidiostat begin in Great Britain.

1966 -- Eugene Kenaga is appointed as Dow's first full-time fish, wildlife, and environmental ecologist.

1967 -- Plant science and animal health businesses are consolidated in a single Agricultural Products Department, and products for human health are realigned in a new Pharmaceutical Products company.

1968 -- Coyden coccidiostat receives federal clearance for sale in U.S. Marketing of Plictran, a new miticide, begins in Italy and Chile. (U. S. fruit growers will not get it until 1971).

1969 -- Sales of Kedlor feed compound, an improved source of nitrogen for cattle and sheep, begin in the U.S.

Keith C. Barrons

Chapter 4

Keith C. Barrons, Weed Control Pioneer

Q.: What task, in all the history of mankind, has absorbed more human energy than any other?
A.: Experts generally agree that this honor (or dishonor) goes to the job of pulling weeds out of the food crops man tries to grow.1

Weed control, one of man's oldest, most important, and most onerous concerns, didn't become a science until the World War II era. Until then it was a job tackled by the farmer with his hoe (one of man's earliest inventions) or his bare hands, the man with the hoe becoming the classic symbol of manual labor in all times historical.

It was only with the discovery of 2,4-D as a weed killer -- the first "selective" chemical that killed the weeds but not the food crop -- that the word "herbicide" came to be known and that chemicals that would kill weeds began to substitute for the hoe.

In August, 1944, a paper was published by researchers at the New York Agricultural Experiment Station announcing that a chemical called 2,4-dichlorophenoxyacetic acid (for obvious reasons generally known as "2,4-D") could be used to kill dandelions and other lawn weeds without hurting the grass.2 The paper immediately caused a hubbub among Dow's research people, because the company was the world's largest manufacturer of phenol, the raw material for making "phenoxies", and the company already had a good deal of know-how in making such compounds. Further, there were no patents involved that would prevent the commercialization of 2,4-D. The door was wide open to anyone who wanted to make it and sell it.

Probably no other scientific discovery has generated as much interest as rapidly at Dow as did the discovery of 2,4-D and the almost immediate availability of the material to the company, put together quickly in their laboratories by Dow chemists for test purposes. Dow was not the first to discover 2,4-D, but it was the first to manufacture it.

Dow's agricultural research staff began field evaluation of their own 2,4-D product in April, 1945, only eight months after the appearance of the New York scientific paper.

Walter C. Dutton, whom Dow had hired away from Michigan State University to run its first agricultural field station, at South Haven, Michigan, made arrangements to use the fairway turf at a local golf course for the many tests that were needed before marketing the material, using varying doses and formulations of it. These tests confirmed that 2,4-D killed off a wide range of common turf weeds without hurting the fairway turf. As one visitor to these plots commented, "Dandelion and plantain just faded away like magic".

Dutton looked about for an assistant to help with this work, someone with experience in this type of activity, and hired Keith C. Barrons, one of his faculty associates at Michigan State, who had evaluated herbicidal formulations there in the early 1940's. The erstwhile Prof. Barrons was soon at work traveling about the U.S. Midwest setting up tests of 2,4-D on a variety of weeds and a variety of crops. /

These showed that 2,4-D didn't bother wheat and other grains, or corn, in dosages that took care of the weeds.

The more testing they did, the better the product looked. "That first year of 2,4-D at Dow was not without its amusing moments", Barrons said later. "During the peak of dandelion bloom, when researchers were elated with good control at modest dosages, a lady golfer scolded them for killing 'all those beautiful flowers'. When a review of the season's findings was given to Dow's Agricultural Sales Group it was suggested that control of many weeds in grain fields could be obtained with as little as a quarter pound per acre. Don Sanford, who was used to selling truckloads of pest control chemicals to orchardists, exclaimed, 'Gosh, we could never make any money with that small a dose'. Don changed his mind when reminded of the vast acreage of wheat and other cereal crops in the U.S. and Canada alone."3

Looking for data on the effect of 2,4-D on fish, Barrons found none, so he made an arrangement with a Michigan State University fish biologist, who agreed to run a test for him if Barrons would supply him with three dozen goldfish from the local variety store. Barron's next expense account included an item, "36 goldfish @ .25 cents, $9.00". When his check came back from the Dow treasurer there was a note attached reading, "Hope you enjoyed the goldfish". Swallowing goldfish was a much publicized student stunt at the time. 2,4-D turned out to be innocuous to goldfish.

By late 1945 the Dow management was convinced that 2,4-D offered it a great opportunity even though much competition was on the horizon. Construction of a production plant got underway and the Ag Sales group geared up to make Dow a leading supplier of not only 2,4-D but formulations of 2,4-D designed for special markets such as railroad and highway maintenance and electric utility transmission, for control of tall-growing woody plants along their rights-of-way.

In late 1947 the pieces began to fall into place and Dow submitted an application to Washington for registration of a 40 percent amine salt formulation it called "2,4-Dow-Formula 40". At the time the U.S. Department of Agriculture was responsible for pesticide registration and with the farming world's keen interest in this new approach to weed control the regulators took surprisingly fast action. Just before Christmas of 1947 registration was granted and Dow was in the 2,4-D business.

2,4-D turned out to be one of the company's longest and best-selling products. In 1998 Dow celebrated 50 years of 2,4-D at a company gathering in Midland, with the product still "going strong". Most pesticides have a commercial life of only a few years.

An early addition to the Dow phenoxy arsenal was a related herbicide called MCPA, 4 which has safety advantages when used in certain grain crops. Another long-lasting sales item for Dow, still in good demand after 50 years, MCPA has been favored by many growers in Canada and Europe.

The discovery of the weed-control power of 2,4-D set off a great flurry of chemical research into related compounds, of which MCPA was only one result. The chemists worked diligently to change, chemically speaking, the phenyl ring substitutions and the aliphatic side chains. Out of this process came 2,4,5-T, to which we shall return in a moment. Combinations of 2,4-D and 2,4,5-T were tried, particularly on woody plants on uitility routes, rail and highway rights-of-way and gave superior overall results.

The company put together a combination of 2,4-D and 2,4,5-T and called it Esteron Brush Killer, and it was a big seller for woody plant control on rights-of-way.

Tinkering with the side chains also revealed a product called silvex, which was useful for woody weeds. (Both 2,4,5-T and silvex were withdrawn from the market later, by order of the government agency EPA, because they contained a trace impurity called dioxin).5

Barrons himself spent a long and productive career at Dow devoted to the development of these kinds of weed-killers and grass-killers and became the first employee distinguished by the title of "developmental scientist".

Aside from 2,4-D, his principal discovery was the grass killer, dalapon, sold by Dow under the trade name, Dowpon. He said he discovered it "by a series of happy accidents".6

"I spent much of June, 1947, in North Dakota putting out trials of 2,4-D for weed control in spring wheat", he recalled. "Before starting for home I stopped at the office of the extension weed specialist at North Dakota State University to thank him for the help he had given us in arranging with local farmers for permission to establish experimental plots on their fields. As I was about to leave, he picked up a bottle off a shelf and said, 'Hey, Keith, what do you know about this experimental grass killer that Dupont just sent me?' I glanced at the label and read 'ammonium trichlor acetate'. As I was in a hurry to catch a train for home (yes, we still rode them in those days), I thanked him for keeping me posted on our worthy competitor's experimental introductions for trial and didn't even have time to read their suggested range. En route home I got to thinking: a salt of trichloracetic acid -- sounds like Dow.

"When I got home, I reviewed the results of our wheat weed-control experiments with Walter Dutton, my boss, and asked if on his trip to Midland later that week he would see if any lab had ammonium trichloracetate on hand that we might acquire for a look at Dupont's discovery. The next Monday he handed me a bottle labeled 'sodium trichloracetate', saying there was no ammonium salt of trichloracetic acid on hand but why not give the sodium salt a try? That day Llewellyn L. (Bud) Coulter, then a graduate student at Michigan State University, who helped me in his spare time with brush control tests with the phenoxies, applied Sodium TCA at a fairly high rate to a small plot of vigorous quack grass. A week later nothing much had happened to the plot so we guessed the ammonium moiety might be essential, or grass only took it up by the roots. Weather had been dry the week following application. I was off to read brush control tests in Pennsylvania for the rest of that week and when I first saw Bud the following Monday he reported that something seemed to be happening on the quack grass plot. A week later we knew that Sodium TCA was a grass killer.

"Later we found the sodium salt and ammonium salt were equivalent at the same TCA level and that uptake was largely by roots. As Dow had made trichloracetic acid at one time or another and approval for non-crop uses was then relatively easy for a compound of modest mammalian toxicity we soon were in the TCA business for railroads, highway perimeters and other non-crop uses.

"What has this to do with Dowpon? Well, the two compounds are closely related. I often wondered if Dupont had done a thorough job of checking other halogenated carboxillic acids for possible grass effects. One would expect a smart research outfit like Dupont to touch all the bases but they claimed only the ammonium salt of TCA for activity as a grass killer in a patent they issued.

"I transferred from the South Haven Field group to the Midland Ag Lab in the spring of 1949. In one of my early sessions with my new boss, G. E. (Lefty) Lynn, I related the TCA story as far as it had developed and speculated that there might be related compounds we should screen. Lefty agreed. A few compounds on shelves were rounded up and Lefty convinced the Britton Lab to put together a range of related compounds varying in the number of carbons and the position of halogen substituents. These were all screened in comparison with sodium TCA.

"I was really excited when a couple of days after application in a weekly routine screening test of new compounds, one seemed to be showing distinct effects on the corn seedlings routinely used in our screening

59

procedure. Needless to say no time was lost in conducting a follow-up test. We were really excited when the experimental material showed clear-cut activity applied to leaves of corn, showing that, unlike Sodium TCA, it was foliar absorbed and translocated, an essential characteristic for a good grass control herbicide. That was what turned out to be dalapon, or Dowpon.

"It didn't take long to have more compound synthesized in quantities adequate for field tests at Midland and South Haven. From there on it was a team effort. The contributors to this effort that I can remember are John Davidson and Andy Watson, who ran the early field tests, Larry Southwick and Chet Otis, who did the early cooperative tests, Hillard Smith, who spearheaded the early marketing, particularly to railroads, Harry Brust, who did the chemistry, and Jim Maddox, who initiated the production process."

Dalapon, called "Dowpon" in the Dow lexicon, became one of the company's star products, and before long the company began to build plants to produce it not only in the U.S. but around the world. The first one outside the U.S. was built at King's Lynn, on the east coast of Great Britain, in 1958.

The King's Lynn plant was built at the behest of Dr. Walter Ripper, a major British beet grower who had learned how effectively Dowpon dealt with quack grass (called couch grass in Great Britain) and other weeds in the sugar beet fields on a visit to Midland, and he proposed to help promote the product throughout the European market and the British Commonwealth. That launched the product on the British and European markets. Dow people learned later on that very little Dowpon was sold in the U.K. and that most of the King's Lynn production was exported to the Middle East and Malaysia. It turned out that Dowpon was the only selective grass killer that could handle a grass that infested the Malaysian rubber plantations. Lalang lalang, or "sword" grass, dospalum conjugatum, so-called because of its sword-like leaf, grows rapidly, and is difficult to cut down. Dow was soon selling 3,000 tons of Dowpon per year to the Malaysian rubber growers. A dozen years later Dow built a Malaysian dalapon plant at Shah Alam, near Kuala Lumpur, to service this market. In 1975 it built another at Medan, in northern Sumatra.

"A major use for it was for Johnson grass control in cotton and various weedy grasses in sugar cane", Barrons said. "It found a good market in Hawaii in the pineapple fields. It got a start in Cuba for sugar cane weeds but Castro came along and spoiled it all -- Wendell Mullison and I were meeting with the Cuban sugar producers association while Fidel Castro was still up in the hills".

Dowpon was also a big hit in removing the weeds in railway ballast. Hillard Smith, Barrons recalled, made an arrangement with John Quarles, who was in the contract railroad spraying business "Quarles had used TCA and we worked with him in an early test of Dowpon", Barrons said. "He purchased the first product as a liquid, shipped in an insulated car, loaded cold. I had the pleasure of being on the spray car that applied the first commercial dalapon solution, the first we had ever sold, on a railroad just south of Miami. John, whom I had got to know quite well, asked me to pull the lever to start the first commercial application of the compound".

"Dowpon may be said to be a very environmentally friendly pesticide", Barrons said. "It has low toxicity to most forms of animal life, short life in the soil, where it breaks down to common substances, and no spray drift problem. Crop yields are increased through good grass weed control. With other Dow products one can say much the same thing. They increase crop productivity, thereby saving acres that may be left in forest or wildlife preserves".

While this was going on at Dow, the U.S. Army -- which in the early days of 2,4-D was fighting in Europe and Asia in World War II -- was also interested in 2,4-D and was screening various members of the phenoxy family at its Fort Detrick, Maryland, research center. Could these new herbicides be used to destroy an enemy's crops by applying them from the air? The army wanted to know, and if possible to possess an anti-crop weapon before its enemies did.

"The thought of applying an herbicide by air (to kill crops) is repellent to most people today", Barrons said, "but old-timers who remember the dark days of 1942, with two enemies seeking our destruction, can understand the U.S. Army's desire for an anti-crop weapon, if one could be found". The army's research determined that some of the chlorophenoxy acetic acids were highly toxic to various crops not members of the grass family, including potatoes and sugar beets. No anti-crop weapon was ever employed, "but if the war in Europe had continued beyond 1945 an acute shortage of potatoes and sugars would probably have occurred in Germany", he said. "2,4-D and its 2,4,5-T analog were prime candidates for such usage".

The controversial product 2,4,5-T, better known as Agent Orange (an orange band was painted around shells containing it to identify them), became famous when it was used during the war in Vietnam to defoliate large areas of trees and deprive the Viet Cong of cover.   It contained microscopic quantities of an impurity called dioxin, and eventually was banned from commerce by the EPA for this reason, along with DDT and all products containing DDT or 2,4,5-T.

In 1953 Barrons became manager of all Dow field research and agricultural chemicals development, and his role in the testing and nurture of new agricultural products in the succeeding years was so much respected and appreciated by his colleagues that one of the formulations of dalapon with other herbicides was named for him. This was Baron (naming a formulation for a person is considered bad practice by "aggie" people, so the word was changed slightly to conceal that fact). Baron combined Dowpon and 2,4,5-T, but was relegated to the bone pile when 2,4,5-T was banned.

The same was true for two other formulations called Novege and Erbon.

Barrons had a long and brilliant career in the development of agricultural pesticides. Born in 1912, he graduated from the University of Minnesota in 1933, earned an M.S. degree in agronomy there, and then took a job as a plant breeder for the W. Attlee Burpee Seed Co., in Philadelphia., where he participated in development of the world's leading lettuce variety and worked on genetic improvements to tomatoes.   He also worked at plant breeding and teaching at the Auburn University and Michigan State University Horticulture Departments, where he became an assistant professor in 1939 and a full professor later, before joining the Dow Chemical Company in 1945. He earned his Ph.D. in horticulture from Michigan State in 1950. He became Dow's Director of plant science research and development in 1961, scientific advisor to the Agricultural

Department's research and development manager in 1968, and the company's first development scientist in 1969. He retired in 1976.7

A prolific writer all his life, he penned a column called "The Man Behind the Hoe" for House Beautiful magazine in the years after his retirement, and also wrote three books dealing with food production and population growth. A compilation in 1969 credited him during his Dow career to that point with 87 technical papers, 75 Dow reports, 37 miscellaneous talks, and 22 newspaper articles (he liked to write "op-ed" articles for the Wall Street Journal and other publications). He had seven patents.

Active in many professional organizations, he served as president of the Agricultural Research Institute, an affiliate of the National Research Council of the National Academy of Science, in 1990. He also had a lifelong interest in the development of farming without plowing and harrowing, and in the mid-1950's did some of the original chemical seedbed preparation work that led to the modern widespread adoption of this practice. The experiments he conducted showed the potential for chemical seedbed preparation without conventional tillage and served as the basis for the growth of this practice in later years. Barrons was named "No Till (as it came to be called) Pioneer of the Year" in 1975 by No Till Farmer magazine in Milwaukee. He himself thought his research work on "no till" farming was possibly his most significant agricultural contribution.

In his writings Barrons pleaded tirelessly for a balanced view of the pesticides and their role. Books such as Rachel Carson's "Silent Spring" (1962), he contended, presented only one side of the question, and too many of the writers engaged in the pesticide controversy also considered only one side of the question.

"The public has become highly sensitive to the problems of chemical pollution from reports about PBBs, PCBs, Love Canal, and other hazardous wastes", as one reviewer of his books said. "In the public's mind, pesticides are a similar hazard, instead of the tools they are -- just as fertilizers, trucks, tractors, cultivators, and harvesters are tools. Barrons has observed from his discussions with the public that most people are 'quite unaware of the proven benefits of pesticides; they had been shown only the negative side of the coin. Wise decisions on trade-offs require knowledge of both sides of a controversy'."8

Probably his most effective work was his second book, "Are Pesticides Really Necessary?" , 9 presented in three parts. The first part,. "Why Pests Have Not Overwhelmed Us", details the ways in which nature's checks and balances work and how humans can manipulate them to some extent. The second part discusses modern pest control technology and the differences it has made in crop protection, conservation of resources and energy, food and fiber production, and control of diseases in domestic animals and humans. The third part deals with pesticide safety.

"Today there are over a half billion acres of small grains in the world", Barrons pointed out, "and even this does not always produce enough, judging by occasional shortages. If we went back to the weed-infested grain of the 1930s we wouldn't be just a little bit short; there would often be a food crisis of considerable magnitude. More than 200 million acres of the world's highest-yielding grain receives a selective spray of 2,4-D, MCPA or other herbicides. These astonishing tools, that make weeds fade away or stunt them beyond recovery without hurting the crop, have increased yields of sprayed acreage by 10 to 20 percent and, on some fields, even more. My estimate is that bread grains that are treated with selective herbicides yield at least five bushels more per acre, making a net increase of no less than a billion bushels annually. Many authorities would say that this is too conservative a figure. That is almost as much wheat as is on hand as a reserve in the world's granaries at the beginning of some harvest seasons. A bushel of wheat will produce enough flour for at least 65 one-pound loaves of bread, so this gain in food supply through the use of selective herbicides gives us the equivalent of 65 billion loaves, nearly 15 loaves for each person on earth". 10

His first book, "The Food in Your Future -- Steps to Abundance" (1975) is a practical guide for increasing the world's food supply "for all who are involved with agriculture and the food industry". Among his other writings is a series of pamphlets, with titles such as "The Positive Side of Pesticides" and "Organic Farming, the Whole Story". "Non-chemical approaches to plant nutrition and past management have merit and those that have proven effective and economically sound are widely used", he wrote in the latter, "but alone they could not provide food for the world's

5.2 billion people. Nor could they assure a sustainable agriculture capable of keeping up with the further growth in population demographers say is inevitable. Let us look at the whole picture, including the agronomically and economically sound aspects of organic methods, but also where they must be supplemented with fertilizers and pesticides."11

His third and final work, "A Catastrophe in the Making" (1991), voiced his growing pessimism for the future. "It is reported that 21 species disappear per day, more than 5,000 acres of jungle are lost per hour, and more than half the world goes to bed hungry at night", he wrote. "More than 40,000 children die of starvation daily. A Catastrophe in the Making". This book makes public for the first time a series of five letters he wrote to Pope John Paul II at this period entreating him to modify his anti-birth control encyclical of 1968, Humanae Vitae. Barrons (who was a Presbyterian elder), based on a lifetime of studies, felt mankind was headed towards a doubling of the world's population but only a 50 per cent increase in the food supply, "which spells a lot of hunger in the 21st century", he said. "Human capacity to reproduce is infinite", he told the Pope. "Planet Earth and its resources are finite". 12

He was still writing at age 91, when he died at Traverse City, Michigan, in March of 2003. His last work was a six-part treatise on the need for immigration reform.13

Robert D. Barnard

Chapter 5

Barney Barnard, Process Whiz

They were consummate professionals, this little band of research scientists in California in the 1930's, but they loved oddball kinds of competition. Every night, wheeling home over the California mountains from the laboratory in Pittsburg, where they worked, towards Concord, where many of them lived, they ran a little contest to see which of their automobiles would coast the farthest downhill with the motor off. The rule was that as you hit the top of Willow Pass you switched off your engine and coasted down the long hill towards Concord, keeping a record of where your car finally stopped. The regular contestants were Chuck Oldershaw, who drove an Oldsmobile with a rocket engine, Barney Barnard, who had a Hupmobile, a make of car long ago relegated to the old car museums, and Bob Heitz, research and development director for Dow in the West.

Barney's Hupmobile seemed to be a better free-wheeler than the others and he usually won.

They were free-wheeling in their research methods as well. Once they were working on a large tank design that didn't seem to function. Why it wouldn't was the mystery, and they puzzled over it for days on end. One morning Barney brought in his wife's vacuum cleaner and a couple of bags of confetti. While his colleagues looked on in amazement he hooked up the nozzle of the vacuum cleaner to a drum and sprinkled confetti into the materials he fed into it. With the confetti whirling around he could immediately trace the flow pattern that was occurring and determine where the material should be introduced into the drum, and he could also determine the best dimensions and speed and temperature. Their problem with the tank design was solved, thanks to a household vacuum cleaner. Those were the days before highly sophisticated equipment was introduced to help researchers solve such problems.

Years later, at his retirement party, Barney's colleagues presented a brand new vacuum cleaner to his wife, "Cookie", in memory of his study of the flow patterns in the chlorination of methane.1

Barney came to the research profession and the Dow Chemical Company by a roundabout route. His parents came from a tiny place called Osawatomie, Kansas, and he himself was born and raised in Evanston, Wyoming, in the mountainous southwest corner of that state. He spent the summer after his graduation from high school on horseback tending to a flock of 2,000 sheep in the foothills of the Rockies, about 40 miles up on the slopes of Mt. Elizabeth. There was just he and a friend whose father owned the flock, their horses, and five sheep dogs. "I had a lot of time to think about my life", he said. "I decided this business of being active politically and being president (he had been a star student and the president of his class three times in junior and senior high school) didn't get anybody any friends and didn't do any good. It didn't produce anything that I was interested in. So I completely bowed out of that kind of activity in college, and became more interested in science and mathematics, and building things, contributing to the world. Not things where I had to order someone around. That was a big changing point in my life."2

From that time on, he avoided situations where he "had to order someone around", and concentrated on inventing things that would "contribute to the world".

He was just beginning his junior year at the University of Wyoming, where he was carrying a double major, in chemistry and mathematics, when he was almost killed in a pedestrian/car accident, "the most traumatic thing that ever happened to me", he called it.

"I was unconscious for a day and a half", he said. "I was crossing the road in front of the girl's dorm with a girl, in a snowstorm, and a guy came up the street and turned into his driveway and I didn't see him and I have no recollection of ever seeing him. Boy, it really nailed me. It dislocated a couple of my lower spine vertebrae. For years if I'd bend over I couldn't get up except by bending my knees. It took all the skin off most of the right side of my face and affected my eyesight so that I couldn't see very well. I had maybe half a dozen changes in glasses in the next six months. The worst thing about it was I always had a real good memory. I could read a lesson and that's all I had to do was read it and after the accident I could study like hell at night and I would get up in the morning and I couldn't tell if I had read it or not. The doctor suggested that I leave school for a year but I figured if I left school for a year I'd probably never come back so I stuck it out. Damn near failed, but I stuck it out. By the next year, I recovered as much as I could".

"When I had the stroke a couple of years ago (Barney was speaking in 1989) they gave my head a catscan and when they got all through the doctor who was doing it walked me carefully out...he said 'there's a massive scar in the back of your head and a quarter of your brain is scar tissue'. He thought the stroke had done it. I told him, 'let's not chase any 50-year-old red herrings'. I'm sure that's what it was. Anyway, I was functional. I spent the next summer after that, between my junior and senior years, working for the Forest Service near Yellowstone Park. They had a program of white pine blister rust control. The plan was to root out and kill all the plants -- currant, raspberry, and gooseberry -- which are alternate hosts of the rust. We were located on Togwatee Pass, southeast of Yellowstone Park at an elevation of 10,500 ft. My back was still giving me fits. One day I was digging a bush out of the side of the hill and it tormented me beyond standing and I just grabbed the root and pulled as hard as I could. I heard a great big pop in my back and instead of killing me or paralyzing me it apparently slid back to where it should have been. In a few weeks most of the ailment was gone".

These were the years of the Great Depression and jobs for new graduates were hard to find. "I wrote over 200 letters of application before school got out and most of the letters I got replies from, but no job" he said. "People were courteous in those days".

That summer he went to visit his uncle John (Barnard), then superintendent of Westwind Farms, a big fruit ranch near Brentwood, California, arriving there at the height of the apricot season. The apricots were cut and dried mainly by Mexican migrants, and the ranch had a Mexican camp with "a couple dozen one-room houses". The season had barely begun when the Mexicans went on strike. The ranch also had a camp of migratory Okies, who did most of the picking. "I organized a crew out of the Okies and we dried 1,100 tons of apricots", Barney said. "God, it was hot! There were weeks at a time that every day the temperature got to 105 to 108 in the shade -- and we were not in the shade, for damn sure. Those guys worked hard and I worked alongside of them, just like one of them".3

Every couple of weeks he would take a day off and visit a list of about 20 of the firms in the area to which he had applied for a job. "I would go around and call on them in Berkeley and Richmond and San Francisco, and they would talk to you, but there just weren't any jobs. Among others I kept visiting Dow (then called Great Western Electrochemical; it was purchased by Dow in 1938 and became that firm's Western Division). In those days the public road drove right through the middle of the plant. You began to smell Dow Chemical Company when you left Antioch. One day Dr. Hirschkind (vice president for research of Great Western) called up and asked me if I would like to have a job. There wasn't much doubt, of course. He said to report in the next day. I can remember asking, 'What should I wear?' The reason I asked that was that half the time when I'd visited there the (research) guys were running around in coveralls. They were obviously working out in the plant, getting dirty..

"When I reported in the next morning, Tom Brown met me and they had a wooden lead-lined box about three feet long and two feet wide that was full of bottles -- wide-mouthed bottles, chemical bottles, brown bottles -- and he said, 'There's the samples and there's the stills'. The stills were mounted on two sawhorses and three planks. 'We need the answers', he said."

His new colleagues told him that it seemed like half the people in the laboratory when he joined it were called "Bob" and one more would be too much, so his name was going to be "Barney". Barnard said that was fine, and he was always called Barney in the company, but it was confusing to his family because he had an uncle known as Barney, and he himself had always been known in the family as "Bob".

When he arrived, "Doc" Hirschkind and his crew were working to perfect the "pertet" process, which involved taking methane gas, which was available in prodigious quantities in the oil fields, and in one step converting it into a variety of chemical compounds, including carbon tetrachloride and perchlorethylene. "Perchlor" became the key chemical used by dry cleaners --- it made dry cleaning safer and quicker and cheaper, and more accessible to the average American family. Possession of the process also became one of the main attractions leading to the acquisition of Great Western by Dow.

"I had never run a fractional distillation in my life", Barney said. "I didn't know anything about it. Boy, I was starting in from scratch". Bob Heitz, who turned out to be his boss, showed him how. "He was a great teacher", Barney said.

He worked most of his career with Heitz and their boss, Doc Hirschkind, the "Wizard of the West", who was at that time one of California's leading scientific minds. 4

"But what a lousy driver he was", Barney said. "He ripped the clutch out of numerous cars. He had no use at all for second or low gears -- he always started out in high. He eternally came to work with a banged fender. He'd get it fixed and the next week he'd have a dent again". A colleague told of going to a meeting with him over in San Francisco, "and he just kept running through each red light. I would say, 'Doc, that was a red light'. He would say, "Yeah, but no one was coming'."

"I think Doc had a soft spot in his heart for me", Barney said, " because early in the war (WW II) Clyde Davis and I had talked it over and decided that we could contribute in the best way by becoming navigators. They could turn out pilots but they couldn't turn out good navigators very fast and both Clyde and I had enough mathematics for it. Clyde got the Air Force Navigator Training Book and we studied it, and we decided that we would join up. Somebody told Doc we were planning to do this and Doc called us in and said that he thought we could contribute more staying here and he talked to the draft board and we got communications which said that we should stay right where we were. And they were plunking those birds in the ocean pretty damn regularly because they didn't have navigators".

With the war coming on he had gotten married. "We were married in Reno", he said. "I came up to Reno and she came down to Reno and we came back to Brentwood with my uncle. He had taken me up. We were married on October 24 and I went to work for Dow on November 6. Heaven smiled on us. We had a fine time". The couple had six children, four girls and two boys, and at the time Barney was interviewed, 50 years later, they had 15 grandchildren.

By the end of the war he had acquired a reputation as a cracker-jack process development man and he was doing that full time.

"On VJ Day everybody got a holiday and they told us about 3:00 in the afternoon that it was to be the next day, so Joel Thompson, Clyde Davis and Larry Leedum and I went up on the opening day of deer season on Dollar Mountain in Lake County and by sunup the next morning we had five deer down. That was VJ Day. I ended up lugging two deer five miles down off of Dollar Mountain in 105 degree heat."

Barney is best remembered nowadays for his contributions in the development of Vikane, Dow's trademark for the insecticide and fumigant, sulfuryl fluoride, widely used in the West and Hawaii for the fumigation of termite-infested houses and buildings.5

"It's hard to get at them (the termites)", Barney said. "Vikane diffuses into the wood well and is very toxic. It only takes about a one per cent concentration in air to kill them. It will kill people at that concentration too. That's the reason for evacuating buildings that are being fumigated, of course.

The product almost never made it to market because of a production problem.

"You couldn't get the chlorine out of the Vikane because of an azeotrope", Barney said. "I discovered you could break the azeotrope by feeding in excess sulfur dioxide. That enabled the separation of chlorine and Vikane -- Vikane has a very low chlorine specification. The trouble was that it (the chlorine) would tarnish and corrode all the metal things like silverware, silver bowls and anything of that nature in the houses they fumigated. So we had that problem to work on and I suggested that we try injecting ethylene because I knew that ethylene liquid phase chlorinates like a charm. That cleaned it up fine".

Barney said that one of the things he remembered most vividly about that episode was that somebody from the sales department in Midland called him up and said, "How did you happen to stumble onto that solution?" "Oh God, that made me mad", Barney said. "I told him, 'You don't stumble onto those kind of solutions; a good chemist knows them.'"

He also initiated the research to produce phenol from toluene and followed that development through to the start-up of a production plant, and he conceived and designed the technique for removing caustic soda from salt in Dow's caustic plants. He perfected the process for manufacturing Dowicil S-13 paint preservative and participated in the development of Tordon herbicide and N-Serve nitrogen stabilizer.

Barney also developed the process for the manufacture of Zoalene, a product that prevents coccidiosis in poultry, invented by a group of his colleagues in the Western Division -- W. E. (Bill) Brown, Guy Harris, and Bryant Fischback. Zoalene was the product that eliminated cocccidiosis, the main disease of poultry, and is generally given credit for starting the trend that put chicken and turkey on the daily menus of the American family. Unfortunately it was supplanted by an even better coccidiostat a few years later, and today it is no longer manufactured.

He was honored with the rank of "associate scientist" in 1970 and retired in 1979. He spent three of the intervening years in New Zealand and Australia, and in New Zealand bought himself a motorcycle. "I always wanted a motorcycle but as long as my family was dependent on me I felt I couldn't take the risk. By that time I had enough put away so that Cookie could take care of herself and Lucinda and the kids were through school, so I shopped around and I liked the looks of that beauty. At that time it held the world speed record for commercial bikes at 10 and 25 kilometers, so I bought it. I lost a yard of hide running the darn thing, but I enjoyed it, particularly in New Zealand. "

Mt. Edgemont, near the Ivon Watkins-Dow installation where he was assigned to work, gave him plenty of workouts on his new motorcycle. "Mt. Edgemont had a network of roads that looked like a spider web", Barney said. "You could go around that mountain 100 times and never take the same route. I went around it a lot of times. Pretty country. That was a very interesting chapter in my life."

His assignment was to provide advanced training for the young engineers at IWD. "They were a bunch of gung-ho, young; sharp engineers", Barney said. "I was very gratified to find out what kind of an education they had and by gosh it was good. But they didn't have a damn idea about

73

the practical uses of their knowledge -- they were just like I was in 1940 when I was a new young engineer."

He became one of the team members of the IWD research group, teaching by doing. "They apparently appreciated it", Barney said. "They gave me a silver pitcher when I left".

After New Zealand he went to Australia and repeated the process. "The societies in the two places are quite different", Barney observed. "New Zealand was peopled by the British Army first, and the army was directed by British gentlemen, and the first settlers were the gentry that had been given huge land grants and they were well-off people, so that the kind of society that got built up was completely different. The Maoris, the New Zealand natives, were never defeated in a war, so they weren't looked down on like the Australian natives, the Aboriginals. In Australia the country was peopled by criminals --- they hauled them over there by shiploads. Some of them were good people of course, but they certainly weren't well educated and gentrified. Some of them hunted the Aboriginals just like they did the kangaroos.

"Cookie and I went on a trip fairly deep into the State of South Australia and we stopped at a place that was a museum. The old caretaker there engaged us in conversation and we talked to him for at least an hour. He told us how they used to organize hunting parties. They would get on horseback and go out and see who could shoot the most natives."

Barney gave Bob Heitz a good deal of the credit for his success. "The thing that impressed me about him", he said, "was that he never told you what to do. He would ask questions, and ask questions, and ask questions, and after you got to know him you would realize that he did not ask idle questions. Quite generally it was something that you were in too much of a hurry to pay attention to. He was just incredible in that he would let you go ahead and make a mistake if it wasn't too bad or dangerous. I think he believed that if you learned it yourself, you would remember it better".

"It's true, too", Barney said.

J. F. Kagy

Chapter 6

John Franklin Kagy and the K-List

Some of his friends knew him as a fine musician and music lover; he was the principal cellist of the Long Beach (California) Philharmonic Orchestra. Others knew him as an enthusiastic fan of deep-sea fishing, ready to go out into the Pacific in search of the big ones at a moment's notice. His workaday colleagues saw an entirely different dimension of his personality, because he was first of all a research chemist and entomologist and probably knew as much about the insect enemies of California agriculture as any man alive. He was director of the Agricultural Research Laboratory of Dow Chemical's Western Division for 24 years.

Formally he was Dr. John Franklin Kagy, but he was a modest man and preferred to be known simply as "Kage" (pronounced "Kaig"). He spent most of his career devising ways of combating the myriad insects, mites, fungi, and assorted other critters that afflict California agriculture, and he was very successful at it. Indeed, it can be said that without his contributions California would probably not be the world's most productive farming area today.

When he retired, in 1972, the California legislature took note of his career and adopted a special Resolution commending his outstanding contributions to California agriculture.1

"Dr. John F. Kagy", the resolution said, "has for the last 35 years been a key figure in the development and use of chemicals to improve California crop yields...was one of the pioneer investigators in the use of organic chemicals as insecticides...pioneered the practice of soil fumigation, was instrumental in the development of Tordon herbicide as well as many other Dow agricultural products, and is credited with numerous patents and publications.....(We) commend him for his pioneering and outstanding research in the field of agricultural pesticides..."

Kage was born in Denver, Colorado, in 1907 but moved with his parents to Des Moines, Iowa, at the age of two when his father, E. O. Kagy, became dean of the pharmacy school at Drake University. His father persuaded him to study pharmacy, and he graduated from Drake with a B.S. in pharmacy in 1929 . But somehow he was unhappy as a fledgling pharmacist, and he soon decided to try something else -- chemistry, maybe, he thought.   He entered Iowa State College at Ames and obtained a B.S. in chemistry there, and a master's and Ph.D. in zoology and entomology.

While he was still an undergraduate at Ames he began to devise new ways to determine the biological activity of chemicals, and this particular interest and skill became the key to his career.   In 1931, as he was graduating with his degree in chemistry, Dow Chemical sponsored a research fellowship at Iowa State and young Kagy, now a graduate student, was awarded the fellowship. Under its terms, with Prof. C. H. Richardson of the Iowa State department of Zoology and Entomology as his supervisor, he worked at measuring the bio-activity of chemical samples sent to him by Dow. He did so well at it that the grant was renewed for six straight years, a godsend for Kagy in the depression era of the 1930s. Dow was one of the extremely rare companies who sponsored such grants, or grants of any kind, in those days.

 At first Dow researchers marked samples of the chemicals to be tested by Kagy with his initials and the number of the chemical to be tested -- "JFK-1", "JFK-2", "JFK-3", etc. (this was many years before John F. Kennedy came to prominence), but the practice became so frequent and popular that a considerable backlog accumulated and it was soon abbreviated to "K", and called the "K List" .

Over the years since 1931 literally thousands of chemical compounds have made the K List, which still flourishes today as a prime research resource for Dow AgroScience researchers at its headquarters in Indianapolis, Indiana.

One of the first chemical curiosities sent to Kagy by Dow, as it happened, was "DN" , a research development of Dow's Organic Research Laboratory in Midland, Michigan, (today known as the Britton Lab), which was to become the first agricultural product manufactured by Dow for the West Coast market.2

In 1937, equipped with a Ph.D., a wife and a family (in 1932 he had married Mary Countryman, a graduate student in Iowa State College's Botany department, and eventually they had four children), he moved to Riverside, California, and a position in the U. S. Department of Agrculture's Citrus Experiment Station there, operated by the University of California. For the next few years he concentrated on the bug problems of the California citrus crops.

"I look back upon this experience as one of the most challenging of all my lifelong events", Kage wrote later. "Al Boyce was truly an inspiring leader".3

The Riverside station was directed by Dr. Alfred M. Boyce, a distinguished researcher, and it was Boyce who discovered that DN was an effective weapon against the red citrus spider mite, one of the worst pests of the citrus industry.4 Boyce came up with a formula of one per cent DN on a flour made of walnut shells, and applied it as a dust to citrus. It worked. Boyce also pioneered improved dusting equipment. Kagy was impressed that Boyce had helped two California industries with the one product -- the citrus growers, whose orchards suffered severe "blasting" due to mites, and the walnut growers, who sorely needed a use for their by-product walnut shells.

Dow entered the agricultural chemical business in California in 1938 with the product Boyce had devised, calling it "DN-Dust". Kagy's early assignment was to improve the product, working on the product with Boyce at Riverside. The manufacturing process was devised by M. F. (Fred) Ohman, then the production manager at Dow's Seal Beach Iodine Plant, with the active ingredient produced in Midland and shipped to Seal Beach for compounding.

Several of Boyce's students moved over to the Dow payroll with the launching of the product. David T. Prendergast took charge of marketing research and application of the product. R. S. (Sid) Braucher and Robert Underhill became field assistants. Larry Gaver became the business manager. The DN-Dust was applied to citrus trees (mostly oranges and lemons) by a large air blower mounted on a truck which moved from tree to tree. DN-Dust was fed into the airstream and literally blown onto the foliage.

The product had two main weaknesses, Kagy said. "It was not a good ovicide, and mites tended to lay their eggs in areas that are difficult to contact by dusting. In consequence control of the mite populations depended on two applications spaced approximately 10 days to two weeks apart, dependent upon weather conditions, in order to pick up the egg hatch....The other problem was phytotoxity (damage to the citrus plants themselves) under high temperatures with little air movement. (This) was not too serious but was not generally condoned by citrus growers".5

The answer turned out to be chemical. "It turned out that the dicyclohexylamine salt of 2-cyclohexyl 4,6-dinitro phenol was at least a partial answer to the defects of DN-Dust", Kagy said. "A product eventually called DN-Dust D-8 was developed which had greater safety under high temperature conditions and better residual activity than DN-Dust."

During its early years the agricultural research program was a kind of sideline for Dow's Iodine plant at Seal Beach, probably the only instance in history of an iodine plant conducting such a program. As of August 1, 1941, however, the two operations were split and the Seal Beach plant became known as the "I & I" plant -- Iodine and Insecticides". Kagy moved to the Dow payroll and was given an old shop building to convert into a laboratory.

The months that followed were some of the most frustrating in Kagy's career. Four months after he began to organize his laboratory, the Pearl Harbor attack by the Japanese occurred (December 7, 1941) and the country was at war. Research supplies became almost impossible to obtain. "Those early days at Seal Beach were very difficult, at times very frustrating, but nevertheless challenging", he wrote later. "Our research priorities were improved by the U.S. government to a 'B' rating because our objectives were aimed at food production. Research then became much easier to accomplish".

One of the early products developed by the lab was called Dow General Weed Killer. Kagy gave credit for its development to Alden Crafts, of the Botany Dept. of the University of California at Davis. "Crafts conducted

80

some very important research on weeds with material supplied by the Dow Chemical Company", Kagy said.6 "He determined that this one chemical, and in particular its ammonium salt, was most active as a contact herbicide. Alden Crafts inspired our agriculturists at Seal Beach to become interested in weed control and pointed to the scope of the problems and the need for weed control chemicals".

A petroleum oil formulation of the phenol was called Dow General Weed Killer and marketed as an all-purpose contact herbicide. A second product, called Dow Selective, a solvent solution of the ammonium salt of the phenol, was used on vegetable crops, particularly in the Salinas Valley.

Dow was now in the weed control business in California.

When the war was over, in 1946, Kagy was given the title of the job he had been filling for most of the war years, and was named director of the agriculture research laboratory of Dow in the West.

One of his major wartime projects was based on the work of M. W. Stone of the USDA Whittier Laboratory, an expert on the sugar-beet wireworm (Limonius californius M.), which was causing major damage to the lima beans that were the primary field crop in Orange and Ventura counties. Stone discovered that ethylene dibromide was very active against this pest, and "was exceedingly helpful in training us on the important field techniques for potential activity for controlling wireworms infesting beans", Kagy wrote. Kagy and an assistant, Robert R. McPherson, developed a petroleum distillate solution of ethylene dibromide which was called Dowfume W-40. Later they developed an improved formula which was named Dowfume W-10. (It contained 10 pounds per gallon of the active component).

These compounds were highly successful and thousands of acres were treated the first year of the product introduction in 1946. This launched Dow into the soil fumigation business and the battle against nematodes.

Kagy engaged as a consultant a USDA researcher in Salt Lake City, Gerald Thorne, who had for years been attempting to control the sugarbeet nematode (Heterodera schactii S.) . "Thorne was of very great help to us in understanding the rather complex problems of nematode control and learning how to characterize the nematode species in the various soils", Kagy said. In 1948 he hired C. R. (Dick) Youngson and sent him to study nematodes under Thorne at Salt Lake City. When he came back to Seal Beach Youngson became deeply involved in nematode research , in the screening of the species and in the search for other active chemicals for their control

In 1946 Walter Carter of the Pineapple Research Institute in Hawaii, an old friend of Kagy's, invited him to visit the Pineapple Research Institute, where they were also doing work on soil fumigants. It was the first of many such visits. In the Hawaiian Islands Kagy also met Maxwell Johnson, the research chief for what is now known as Del Monte Foods, at their Wahiawa Plantation on Oahu. Johnson, Del Monte's "father of research", had pioneered the use of chlorpicrin as a soil fumigant for pineapple soils and this was part of their standard practice. Kagy told Johnson privately about Dow's experiences with ethylene dibromide.

"As it turned out, Johnson developed the know-how for the use of ethylene dibromide as a soil fumigant for pineapple culture and it became a plantation practice", Kagy said. "The details were a closely guarded secret for years".

Dow's early soil fumigants were followed by another successful product, Fumazone, an invention of A. W. (Art) Swezey.[7] A solid, non-fumigant nematicide was developed by Dick Youngson and called Nellite.[8]

Kagy always encouraged a kind of rivalry between his research crew at Seal Beach and the research crews at Dow's main plant and laboratories in Midland, Michigan. "He preferred that the Snowbirds, as he called us Midland headquarters people, not come west of the Rockies", said Julius E. Johnson, corporate vice president for research and development in the latter years of Kagy's career. "If we did he urged his group not to report more to us than was needed. He was a superb motivator but fiercely loyal to the Western Division organization, his primary line of reporting. Since Seal Beach was in the Los Angeles area they could take visitors and entertain them with many evening diversions there. Using a platoon system on successive evenings, an unsuspecting visitor could be worn down".

It was a matter of pride for Johnson that he helped to change this.9

In 1957 the California work expanded to include a 17-acre field station near Sacramento, and in 1962 to a 125-acre field station near Davis, California. Here Dow researchers cultivated crops representative of California agriculture and carried on the field research necessary to obtain registration for the new products it was developing. The Davis Field Station was particularly active in the early research on Tordon herbicides and N-Serve nitrogen stabilizer.

In 1968 Dow decided to consolidate its West Coast research operations at a big, brand-new laboratory at Walnut Creek, not too far from its main California manufacturing facility at Pittsburg. Kagy rather sadly closed down his beloved old Seal Beach laboratory and moved to the Walnut Creek Research Center. During the final years of his career he served as Science Advisor to the company's Agriculture-Organics Department with the assignment of exploring new areas of potential for Dow technology.

When he retired in 1972 his colleagues from around the world -- for by this time the products he had helped develop were being used worldwide -- gathered at Walnut Creek to pay him the honors they felt he was due. "His contributions to the field of agricultural science cannot be gauged in years of service or even in numbers of inventions (there were many) but rather in the ideas he nurtured, encouraged, and brought to reality in his own mind and in the minds of those with whom he worked", commented Julius Johnson.

"Kagy's thinking is not circumscribed by the limitations of chemical symbols but rather he looks at a problem, determines a need, and looks for a solution, wherever it may be", Johnson said. "Dr. John F. Kagy is a professional".10

Eugene E. Kenaga

Chapter 7

Eugene E. Kenaga, ecologist

Gene Kenaga had two loves, chemistry and nature, and he made a career out of combining these two things as successfully as anyone in his generation.

He grew up in a chemical family -- his father, Ivan, was superintendent of Midland's big Bromine Plant at Dow Chemical for many years -- and went off to the University of Michigan, from which both his father and mother had graduated.

Instead of enrolling in chemistry he signed up for forestry. "I always liked trees", he said, "Still do. I had strong naturalist inclinations. I used to go out on field trips with Bobby Dreisbach, who in addition to being one of the key inventors of styrene plastic was also one of the world's great wasp experts. He got me started on insects. I found out that forestry was a pretty stale business. There wasn't much call for it and there were too many people involved. So I went to the University of Michigan biological station at Douglas Lake and took entomology. By my senior year I had decided to be an entomologist".1

In 1939 he went to the University of Kansas for a year to earn his master's degree, which was in taxonomy (identification of insects). Then he came back to Midland and applied for a job at Dow, "and they hired me", he said. "They were just beginning their expanded agricultural chemicals business, and they were beginning a lot more research. I was very fortunate".

"Quite a few chemical companies were in the insecticide business by 1940", he said. "Monsanto, Merck, Cyanamid, Shell, and a number of others. It was a fairly new field, though, as far as testing organic chemicals was concerned. There weren't very many screening programs. They were making use of compounds that were already in existence."

When World War II came on, he said, "I could have stayed at Dow through the whole wartime without being drafted, but I got a letter asking for entomologists in the Navy, and I decided to go into the Navy". His wartime assignment had to do with grain fumigation.

"There were large stores of grain necessary during the war", he explained. "No one knew when we might need them for war purposes. There were immense Quonset huts and storage bins of grain all over the central United States that were being infested by insects. In order to get rid of the insects, you either had to take the grain through a series of siftings and treat it, or put something on top of the grain and let it go down and kill the insects. At the time they had mixtures of carbon tetrachloride and carbon bisulfide which would penetrate the grain, but the insects on the top surface (where most of the insects were) weren't killed. So Fred Fletcher and I invented a mixture with ethylene dibromide in it (I used my father's ethylene dibromide) that worked very well and Dow went into the EB-5 business, which was the name of that grain fumigant. Fred and I were issued a patent in 1946. EB-5 was used for many years, until the long-term effects of these things were more thoroughly studied and it was banned. Now they don't know what to do with insects in grain sometimes. The elevators are often in bad shape. That was a contribution that Fred and I made to the war effort".

Later he was "shipped out" to Okinawa, and put in charge of malaria control for the northern districts of Okinawa. "On Okinawa", he said, "they had a lot of malaria, and I was there when the atomic bombs were dropped. The Japs were still shooting at us, so I didn't feel too comfortable. That's the first place I used DDT. DDT was the miracle insecticide of World War II, as you probably know. I rode up in a plane, we had brand new compositions of it for airplane spraying and we flew real low over the land. There were all sorts of outdoor binjos (toilets) on Okinawa, and the plane went over with DDT, and in about five or six hours it went from a buzzzzzzz to just quiet. It was really astounding".

DDT "turned off" the insects on Okinawa beautifully, miraculously, he said. "It wiped out the head and body lice, and ticks and fleas. It was marvelous. A lot of deaths from disease would have occurred without it".

When he came back to Midland, Dow put him in charge of raising insects that were representative of the pest insects of the world. "We took a moth and a beetle and an aphid, and things that were entirely different in their morphological aspects to test as representatives of insect classes. Dow was beginning to make things that they thought might be insecticides on purpose. Dr. Edgar C. Britton's laboratory was the main laboratory from which those things came, for a long time. But right after the war, Henry Tolkmith came from Germany, where he had worked with parathion and other phosphate insecticides. They were quite toxic to humans. We were trying to find things that were very good on insects but not so toxic to humans. Korlan (also called Ronnel) was an example of that. That was so safe it was even used on cattle, treating the cattle both internally by translocating in the blood and killing the flies on the outside -- a systemic material".

One of his early successes was development of a fumigant product called Vikane, Dow's name for sulfuryl fluoride. "Methyl bromide was a good fumigant, and Fred Fletcher and I began to develop it for house fumigation", he said. "When we were doing that, we had to make the building pretty tight, so we began to develop tents and things that would cover a whole house to contain the gas. Most houses were too leaky to hold it long enough to do the job. The big use for it was for termites, and the commercial termite problems were mainly in California and Florida. The weakness with methyl bromide was that it reacted with sulfur-containing materials to form mercaptans, which smell bad, and a lot of women's bras were padded with such materials, for example, and they stunk something awful. Also, the mats that were placed underneath rugs were made of materials like that at that time, so the house would stink until they got rid of the mats. The odor would last for years.

"There were two ways to overcome that", he said. "One was to remove all those kinds of things from the house, which wasn't very convenient, and the other was to develop a new material, which is what we were trying to do. I was doing tests that tried to show the ability of a fumigant to penetrate through things. Methyl bromide would penetrate through cardboard packages and kill insects, so it was good from that standpoint. But there were still a lot of difficult problems. Vikane, sulfuryl fluoride, was very volatile. I asked for it to be made, and a Dow chemist named Bob Ruh made it, in 1953 , I think, and since it was an old compound, it was my patent. I had figured from its physical and chemical properties it might be good for that purpose, and it turned out that it was. We started making it about 1957. The patent was issued in 1959. It's now the main thing that's used for termites in Hawaii, California, and Florida. It's still a big product for Dow"

Plictran, an acaricide -- an acaricide is something that kills mites -- was another of his discoveries. "The trend in the 1950s was to be more pinpointed on what kind of critter you killed", he said. "Mites are not an insect, so they have quite a different physiology than most insects. We got into an agreement with M & T Chemicals Inc. to test tin compounds. 2 We found that the trialkyl tin compounds would burn foliage and therefore were not useful for that purpose. But I got to thinking about the size of the molecule, and if the molecule was large enough in size, it might not penetrate the foliage. I had them make tricyclohexyltinhydroxide, a very bulky tin molecule, and it didn't penetrate. It also killed the egg stage of mites, mainly, although also the adult of the mite, which was then a novel way of killing mites. It killed the eggs, and it was used commercially for quite a few years. Dow had two ovicides that were commercial. The other one, Ovotran, was another of my inventions, patented with Richard W. Hummer in 1950.

"Then somebody did some tests which showed some toxicity at high, high dosages, and Dow didn't let us spend the money to go through the millions of dollars of tests that they wanted us to do over again. The EPA had this way of letting us get by with tests that were okay at that time, but then a new test would come along or a slight variation in the test method, and you had to do it all over again. We had to do this on chlorpyrifos, for example. Four stages of tests, which were okay at the time, were later declared invalid, because the volume of the compound picked up so much that they showed more concern then. But Plictran was a good one for quite a while."

Chlorpyrifos, sold by Dow under the name Dursban, 3 which became the world's largest-selling insecticide, was his "pride and joy", he said. "Dow got into making heterocyclic compounds under Ted Norton, and Ray Rigterink was working for him. I had a lot of interest in physical and chemical properties of compounds. I was correlating all sorts of things like that. My best contribution to science was that: the correlation of chemical and physical properties with dissipation in the environment and toxicity. That was my favorite subject. I drew the structure of chlorpyrifos out in relationship to Ronnel, which was a 2,4,5-

trichlorophenyldimethylthiophosphate, and all we did was replace the nitrogen in the phenyl ring. That turned out to be a fantastic thing. It wasn't as biotoxic, and immediately we saw the (insecticidal) activity. Keith Barrons brought up some chinch bugs, the tiny little insect that gets on grass in Florida. They were a big problem down there, and Dow could find an immediate market for this insecticide. It just ruined the grass down there, so I tried that out right away and it killed them. We thought, 'Well, we'll go into control of aquatic insects such as mosquito larvae', and it killed them at parts per billion, so this was really exciting. It was in 1962 that we first tested this insecticide. Now it's the most widely used insecticide in the world, I understand. I think Dow sells at least half a billion dollars' worth of it every year, and more than that most years. But it didn't get that way easily. It was a long, hard fight. I put chlorpyrifos into Dow's development system first, to have it field tested. Then when I got into the environmental area, in 1966, in registration of pesticides, I was the one who took it through the EPA regulations to get it approved for the environmental effects of insecticide uses. So I was with the development of chlorpyrifos for quite a while, from beginning to end.

"In the meanwhile, the sales people got good at promoting it. Dow wasn't very good at promoting things in the sales area for a long, long time. It's true. We lost out on a number of compounds simply because of that".

He was instrumental in the development of Dow's screening process for insecticides, which rapidly became one of the best in the business. "We started out kind of small with three or four insects", he said, "and then we enlarged our research into the household insect area, and we were screening against about fifteen different species. We were the first company to screen against aquatic organisms. We were the first to screen against Daphnia, which is an invertebrate organism, which kind of represents mosquitoes. We were the first to screen against snails, and I was the contact for Dow with the World Health Organization on molluscicides, which carry schistosomiasis (sleeping sickness). We were trying to help develop materials that would control that in the Nile river and Puerto Rico and tropical places like that. We had fish in there, too. So we were actively interested long before any other company, really, in doing the sorts of tests that cover the spectrum that the EPA was interested in. Not only were we doing the work on those things, but the Dow herbicide people were screening aquatic plants and agricultural plants, so we had a spectrum of 30 or 35 species of organisms that many thousands of compounds went through on screening".4

He remembered a marine paint developed by the company that was never sold. "In 1970, when the EPA had just been formed, we were working with M & T Chemicals, who made triethyltin compounds. I don't remember which one it was, chloride probably, but it would dissipate into the water from the treated boats and kill organisms close by. Nearly all the ships in the world were being painted with that material at the time, and it was affecting shrimps and all sorts of things in the harbors, and we just decided we weren't going to take on the hazards of promoting environmentally unsafe products."

In all, he amassed 30 patents for pesticides, fumigants, acaricides, and related compounds. In the meantime he was also an active pioneer in the environmental movement, forming the Midland Nature Club and serving as its first president in 1953, and then forming the Chippewa Nature Center and serving as its founding president as well. (It is now one of the biggest and best nature centers in the state). In the 1940's he became an enthusiastic bird watcher, and was president of the Michigan Audubon Society in 1962-64. "When I started my bird watching in the 1940s, I was the only active bird watcher in town", he said. "Now there are hundreds of them. I didn't exactly get razzed about it, but I got a lot of questions. People would call me up all the time and ask me what to do about their robins, and all sorts of stuff". In the 1950s he was chairman of the Michigan Audubon Society's conservation committee, which worked to obtain legislation outlawing the killing of hawks and owls. He was instrumental in some of the early efforts to preserve wildlife habitats, getting petitions from Midland, Bay City, and Saginaw and going to the Michigan Department of Conservation to ask for a wildlife sanctuary in the Tobigo lagoon (in Saginaw Bay) and for a state naturalist to be stationed at the Jennison Nature Center in Bay City.

"They granted all those things", he said. "The very first naturalist in the state park system in Michigan was in Bay City, half-time. Those sanctuaries still exist, and they're marvelous for nesting and migratory birds. I helped to save Tawas Point, too, while I was president of the Michigan Audubon Society. It would have been a camping and swimming beach and now it's left as a natural point; it's like a small Cape Cod. It's one of the most marvelous wildfowl spots in the state".

His presidency of the Michigan Audubon Society occurred at the time in 1962 when Rachel Carson published her famous book, "Silent Spring", generally considered now to mark the birth of the modern environmental movement. "I was heavily involved in that", he said. "I caught the flak from both sides. In Audubon I was seen as a chemist, and in Dow I was seen as a naturalist or environmentalist. I could never see taking either extreme side of the pesticide controversy. There were extremes on both sides, and I published bird papers against the extremists on both sides. Rachel Carson's book was extreme on one side, and it certainly led to thoughts that should be pursued, and were pursued, ad infinitum. There's always some professor that picks up the ball and gets a lot of grants for his school because he can make a big statement about how bad something is, and there's always another side, usually an agricultural chemical person, or rarely a professional, who will deny all these things. There could be some truth in between".

All in all, he felt the changes inaugurated by Carson's work have been "a good thing". "We certainly quit putting DDT and PCBs and all those persistent chemicals in the Great Lakes on purpose", he said. "Unfortunately, the environmental groups don't understand the difference between putting new chemicals in and having old ones that they can't remove; taken out. I was on the International Joint Commission of the Great Lakes Committee a few years ago, and they claimed they wanted to have industry's input, but they really didn't. And they're still that way".

In 1960 he was promoted to associate scientist, and then in 1966 he was appointed to be Dow's first full-time ecologist. Julius Johnson, Dow's vice president, research and development, and Keith C. Barrons, director of agricultural chemical research, were responsible for this, he said. "They needed somebody in Dow to follow the testing of Dow chemicals for environmental effects and to be an advisor through them to the board of directors".

"They kind of shifted me gradually, because of my naturalist interests", he said. "When I was president of the Michigan Audubon Society, it was quite interesting to them that a Dow person could be in that position.

During the time before the EPA (which came into being in 1970), the U.S. Department of Agriculture was in charge of the registration of pesticides, so I had to interact with them and develop test methods. You couldn't just say, 'My pesticide is great'. You had to say how it compared with other pesticides and you had to show what test methods you used to yield your results. In those early days in 1964, there weren't any official test methods for wildlife.

"Julius Johnson had contacts with the Denver U.S. Fish and Wildlife Service. We were submitting compounds to them to test the effects on control of birds, pest birds like blackbirds and sparrows, and finally he put me in charge of that. I was keeping track of bird toxicity and selecting the candidates that were to go out there. Well, they were also interested in things that would kill blackbirds but not some other species, so specificity was of interest. I was into that program, and then I was the Dow contact person with the World Health Organization. I was selecting insecticides for them to replace DDT for malaria control. These activities, plus the fact that I was head of the screening program for insecticides, gave me an advantageous position to select things for those programs. I think Julius Johnson was a far-sighted person, and he went against a lot of people in Dow, too, to do all those environmental things, because some people might not have wanted to know all the adverse properties of commercial products. And Keith Barrons was the same way as Julius. So I was given the freedom to do just about anything I wanted to do".

He was also in charge of liaison with the U.S. Department of Interior's research laboratories. "There was a station in Florida that was beginning to test insecticides, there was a station in Patuxent, Maryland, that was doing the bird work, and Denver was doing bird work. I would sample out Dow's agricultural chemicals to them first. This was a matter of seeing how safe Dow agricultural products were to those wildlife organisms."

As the company's ecologist he became active in and interacted with most of the world's leading environmental and ecological groups and societies. "When the EPA was born, they asked all sorts of people for information, and they would hold seminars and be specific about what topics they wanted to talk about, and I was invited to a lot of those", he remembered. "The EPA sponsored the beginnings of some organizations, and one was the ASTM, the American Society for Testing and Materials. It was usually for things like concrete and all sorts of official test methods to test things. Well, they started creating biological test methods, and they sponsored science seminars. Test method development was very important then; that was the name of the game with them. The EPA encouraged the development of these methods, and I became the chair of the bird, mammalian and wildlife toxicology test methods. The book, Avian and Mammalian Wildlife Toxicology, was a collection of papers given at the first symposium, of which I was the editor. That was for test methods which were the bulwark of the way EPA would accept any kind of a test result. They depended upon the test methods developed at ASTM for their regulations.

"We finally decided that the only way to handle the EPA was to have an impartial group that could react with them. The ASTM wasn't that. They were a private organization, not a professional organization. We went to the Society of Toxicology, but they might have one or two wildlife or chemical papers a year. We talked to the Society of Ecotoxicology in Europe, which I had been going to, and they were almost a hundred percent mammalian toxicologists. We went to the Society of Ecology, and they weren't even active. We went to the Entomology Society of America, and you couldn't get them to talk about wildlife. So there wasn't any organization addressing the environmental fate of chemicals, both from the standpoint of dissipation and from toxicology. Just didn't have anything.

"So a man named Richard E. Tucker and a few others of us decided that we needed an organization that could make environmental risk assessments. We sent out letters to see if we could financially support an organization like that. The results were very positive, so we went ahead on an ad hoc basis. Our position was that we had to have equal representation from universities, from government, and from industry on the board of directors and on the committees, so that they couldn't say that there wasn't a discussion with all sides represented. I was selected as the pro tem president and then elected as the first president. The Society of Environmental Toxicology and Chemistry, or SETAC, now has a large European chapter, and we have a lot of chapters in the United States. We have over 3,000 members, and they're chemists, toxicologists, geologists, engineers -- all sorts of people who have to interact to solve environmental problems. We have annual meetings attended by 2200 or 2300 people every year. We are called upon to testify before the Senate and House committees. We have a representative now who is science advisor to the important environmental committees of the U.S. House and Senate. SETAC pays for them to be there. We also have an educational foundation. I'm on the board of directors".

At the age of 60 he finally obtained the Ph.D. that he had wanted in his youth. "The National Academy of Science sent me to a U.S.-Japan seminar on pesticides in Japan in 1971", he said, "and the Japanese kept calling me 'Doctor'. I said 'I'm not a Doctor', but they kept on calling me that, like the polite way the Japanese are."

Two or three years later his Japanese friends invited him to participate in a doctoral program at Tokyo University "for Americans who don't have a Ph.D. but have made notable contributions to science". In 1976, after doing the work involved, he finally received a parchment scroll attesting to his attainment of a Ph.D., one of two Americans so honored. His thesis concerned the environmental work he had done on chlorpyrifos. A Japanese friend wrote him, "Now you won't have to worry about being called 'Doctor'."

In 1979 he was promoted to research scientist, the highest scientific rank at Dow, and continued to serve as the company's liaison to the ecological world at large for the remainder of his career, until he retired at age 65 in 1982..

Among his honors were the founder's award of SETAC, the American Chemical Society's Award for Creative Advances, the Outstanding Conservation Effort Award of the Daughters of the American Revolution, and the Dow company's Community Service Award.

His supervisors at Dow over his 40 years there -- Don Irish, Fred Fletcher, George E. (Lefty) Lynn, Julius Johnson, Keith Barrons, Oscar H. (Trip) Hammer, and Don McCollister -- all gave him an extraordinary degree of freedom, he said. "A lot of Dow people had (that kind of) freedom. All those people let me do just about anything I wanted to do. I was lucky to have such supervisors".

Etcyl Blair

Chapter 8

Etcyl H. Blair, ambassador

In the spring of 1962 a lady named Rachel Carson published a small book called "Silent Spring", and after that nothing was the same for people in the pesticides business.1

Carson, a long-time researcher and editor for the U.S. Fish & Wildlife Service, envisioned a world in which no more robins sang and no more trout leaped in plashy streams, because they had all been killed off by the pesticides used by the world's farmers. This process would eventually result, she asserted, in what she called a "Silent Spring". Her stance was based largely on a study of the shells of wild birds' eggs indicating that pesticides accidentally ingested by birds were causing their eggshells to be thinner than normal, with a consequent danger that their birdlings would not hatch, or if they hatched, would not survive. Slowly, over time, she concluded, pesticides were destroying the bird population, and perhaps the fish as well. A half-century later the eggshell studies are still being debated, and the evidence indicates that most bird species are not really affected.

Seldom in history has a small book had as large an impact, world-wide, as this one did. Rachel Carson is generally given credit for single-handedly launching the environmental movement and its political friends the "greens" with it, and also for giving a big boost to the then budding birding movement. Her book is also credited with giving a giant push to the development of the "organically grown" food industry. Chemicals, and especially pesticides, were suddenly considered by many a threat and an enemy to health and safety, as a result of her book. Almost overnight the bug fighters at Dow and other firms found themselves being attacked, more and more violently as time went on, for all manner of activities. What came to be known as "junk" science (science based on flimsy evidence) came into vogue, and old-time sobersides science was more or less ignored.

Many of the leading national (and international) environmental advocacy organizations were formed at this time, ranging in their views from moderate to radical, with the balance weighted heavily on the radical side.

The public was suddenly willing to accept all sorts of wild stories about chemicals, pesticides being among the worst of the lot. The permissive cultural atmosphere of the 1960's and the war in Vietnam added fuel to the fire, and eventually concentrated the nation's attention on Agent Orange (whose active ingredient was essentially 2,4,5-T, called Agent Orange by the military forces, which painted an orange band around the containers to identify it), used in Vietnam to defoliate the forests and deprive the Viet Cong guerilla fighters of some of their hiding places. Agent Orange quickly became a subject of widespread controversy.

Dow Chemical, a leading producer of 2,4,5-T, was immediately embroiled in this imbroglio as one of the half-dozen or so firms that produced Agent Orange for the military forces during the war in Vietnam. The critics of Agent Orange concentrated their fire on the fact that 2,4,5-T contains a trace impurity called dioxin, and that was the beginning of the dioxin controversy that is still going on, a generation later. Dioxin, they declared, is the most toxic substance known to man, although no human death or illness has ever been traced to it aside from a kind of acne, called "chloracne", that occurs in severe cases.2

"It (the dioxin controversy) started with Agent Orange, but it really came out of the 1970 Hart Commission Hearings (so called for Sen.Philip Hart, of Michigan, who presided) in Washington, D.C." said Etcyl Blair, who was at that time research director for Dow's Agricultural Chemicals Department.3 "That was when Julius Johnson (Dow vice president for research and development) first revealed that dioxins may appear as impurities in the preparation of certain chlorinated phenols. V.K. Rowe (chief toxicologist of Dow) and I accompanied Julius at the hearings. The Bionetics Laboratory employed a scientist named Jacqueline Verett, who had injected 2,4,5-T into chick embryos and in this way produced monstrously deformed chicks. She was to testify, as was Sam Epstein (of the University of Illinois, a leading dioxin activist). The meetings lasted all day and when it was time for Julius to give his testimony, I heard a chirping sound coming from the hall. Chirp, chirp, chirp, chirp, it went. I'll never forget it. 'What in the world is going on?' I thought. Others present also noticed the chirping. At the proper time Sam Epstein, Verett, and others came into the hearing chambers pushing carts loaded with caged chickens. This was my first exposure to Sam Epstein. The chickens were all deformed. Verett removed them from the cages and placed them on the table in front of Sen. Hart and his staff. They all jumped up from their seats and moved away. One chicken landed on Hart's arm and I remember him trying to brush it off. The place went bananas. 'What is going on?', I wondered. 'How do you bring order out of this chaos?' 4

"When it was time for Julius Johnson to make his presentation, no one was interested. It was late in the afternoon, the excitement was over, the press had their story and were gone. The damage had been done.

"I have often wondered what would have happened if Julius had never said (when we first told him about the problems with 2,4,5-T),'Maybe it's due to an impurity, a dioxin'. After all, something did damage the chickens, but injecting 2,4,5-T into the embryos is hardly a sound method to test toxicity. Most biologists reject this method of testing. It is interesting to note that the press was there to record the chicken episode but were gone when Julius gave his presentation. We watched it all on TV that night with disbelief".

After the experience at the Hart hearings, Johnson asked Blair to organize a dioxin program in the company. "I, in turn", Blair said, "enlisted the help of Warren Crummett and his analytical scientists and we travelled to Washington, D.C., to Harvard, and all over the world giving programs and speeches on dioxins. We attended ACS meetings to develop symposia on the subject. Eventually the government and the EPA became very active in dioxin analysis".

When he was back in Midland, Blair said, "I felt that Dow and the chemical industry should publish all the information they had on dioxins and make it a part of the open literature. I identified a number of scientists in Dow, from other companies, from universities, from government, and made arrangements with the ACS (American Chemical Society) to hold a conference on dioxins and to publish a book using the papers presented at the conference. They agreed, and that book was published in 1973."5

"The real heroes with the dioxins", Blair said, "were the analytical scientists at Dow, especially Warren Crummett. Fortunately, in the early days V. K. Rowe and his associates in the Toxicology Laboratory had observed chloracne among some Dow workers in the trichlorophenol plants. Dow did have workers who had developed chloracne, but those problems had been worked out by the manufacturing and process people, with help from the medical department and the tox lab. There were no lasting effects on the people exposed. Dow did notify other companies about the chloracne problems, and a meeting was held in Midland involving our production people, our medical doctors, and our toxicologists.

"When certain chlorinated phenols are heated to high temperatures in the presence of caustic soda", he explained, "two molecules of the chlorinated phenols condense, or react with each other, resulting in the formation of dioxins. The high temperatures and caustic conditions are required in both the formation of the chlorinated phenols and in the preparation of the herbicide 2,4,5-T, which was used in making Agent Orange.....The dioxins appear as impurities in trace quantities only and no serious problem has ever been proven. Dioxin became a burning issue, and remains as such today. The paper industry, for instance, is faced with dioxin problems -- they're being forced because of dioxin to move away from chlorination as a means of treating wood pulp. Very low levels of chlorinated dioxins can be detected in the treatment baths and in certain paper products. And [the dioxin problem] is also the basis for the attempt to ban all uses of chlorine".

Crummett and his colleagues in the Dow analytical laboratories developed a theory that dioxin occurs everywhere there is fire, which turned out to be true. "The 'chemistry of fire' project was an attempt to show that dioxin is everywhere", Blair said. "I don't think it ever did what they wanted it to do. They hoped that by getting samples from volcanoes, from automobile exhaust, from power plants, and a lot of other places, and showing that dioxins were present in all these places, that they could defuse the dioxin issue at Dow. They even heated table salt (sodium chloride) with an organic material and were able to make dioxins at detectable levels. But outside of a curiosity factor, [the chemistry of fire theory] never made much headway with the federal agencies, with the environmental activists, nor with the press."

In spite of the scientific evidence that dioxins do indeed occur everywhere, Blair said, "I think they just couldn't make it go away. It's kind of like terrorism, it won't go away. I am convinced that people like the Sidney

Wolfes (a Ralph Nader aide and dioxin activist) and the Sam Epsteins will not be deterred. I don't care how much data you develop to show that it's not an issue. They have to have their issues, otherwise they don't exist. That's the only thing they live for, to keep pushing their agendas. They're going to do their thing. The Sam Epsteins won't go away. They have nothing else to sell, and there's a certain percentage of the population who listen to these kinds of people. It's important to develop technical information, because then you can tell yourself you have some data on which to stand to support your principles. The Dow scientists did marvellous work. The Dow analytical and toxicological laboratories are second to none in the world. People come from all over the world to find out how Dow did those studies.

"There's now an institute in Bayreuth, Germany, for example, that deals with nothing but dioxins", he said. "They have found dioxins everywhere in Europe, in smokestacks, in their coal-producing factories, and in many different industries. But it doesn't really change anything in the politics of dioxins in the United States. The analytical tools have become so powerful that the smallest numbers that one can imagine are the levels that are being detected. To the public the smallness of the numbers is meaningless. It's kind of like the dollars associated with our national debt. Their bigness makes them meaningless".

-o0o-

Etcyl H. Blair was born in Wynona, Oklahoma, in 1922 and grew up in Winfield, Kansas. Etcyl was a family name, he said. He began playing the violin when he was eight (his father was a country fiddler), and classical music became a lifelong passion. His other great interest was chemistry, and, following a couple years of military service in World War II, in the U.S. Air Force, he earned a degree in chemistry at Southwestern College and then did post-graduate work in organic chemistry at Kansas State University.6 "Kansas State was a big agriculture school, and I was able to obtain a very interesting project doing chemical research on crops of interest to Kansas", he said. "I worked on the isolation and characterization of natural products from alfalfa and various other crops of Kansas. I obtained my master's degree and doctorate from this work".

101

In 1951, the year he earned his Ph.D., he joined the Dow Chemical Company at Midland, Michigan as a research chemist in the agricultural synthesis group of its organic research laboratory. He chose Dow, he said, partly because he and his wife much preferred small-town life, but mostly because it had a symphony orchestra. He began playing violin in the Dow Symphony Orchestra (the company at that time had a Music Department which included a symphony orchestra) in 1951.

He was promoted to group leader and head of the agricultural synthesis group in 1956, becoming almost from the start a specialist in the development of organophosphorus pesticides. He was instrumental in the development of ronnel (also known as ET-57, as Trolene, and by other names), for insect and cattle grub control, Zytron, a crabgrass killer, Ruelene, an animal systemic insecticide, and Nellite, a water-soluble nematicide.

"From a selfish and personal point of view", he said, the event that most pleased him during his Dow career was his involvement with Dursban. "Today it is the world's most used organophosphate insecticide, and I take some satisfaction from having been part of its discovery and development. I feel good that I did something useful which I was hired to do". In all, he was credited with 23 patents.[7]

He moved up to director of the Britton Research Lab (as the organic research lab was now called) in 1967, and a year later was named director of research for the agricultural department of Dow.

His entry into the public arena, as the principal Dow spokesperson for agricultural matters, came about through Malcolm E. (Mac) Pruitt, who had succeeded Julius Johnson as Dow's director of research and development. "Late one day Mac Pruitt phoned me", Blair said. "He said that Dow had been subpoenaed to appear at an OSHA (Occupational Safety and Health Administration) hearing in Washington, D.C., on 13 carcinogens and that he wanted me to take control of the problem and to prepare for the presentations in Washington. I was stunned. I didn't even know what the products were. I knew what OSHA was, but the products involved were not related to ag-- they had nothing to do with our department. The ag products were registered through the Department of Agriculture and through EPA and FDA (Food

& Drug Administration). Ag didn't have OSHA problems. The Department of Agriculture had to approve the use of our products and their safety was regulated by EPA.

"We had about a week to get prepared. Dow made three of the 13 carcinogens in question, one in Texas and two in Michigan. We had two outside lawyers to assist us and Donna J. Roberts was our inside legal adviser. She was assigned to go with us to Washington and was to remain on the project until it was resolved. I decided we should make a technical presentation, because we had a lot of toxicological data in support of our products. It soon became obvious, however, once we were on the scene, that this was not a forum for a technical presentation. The hearing was purely political, and the opposing lawyers attempted to make us look like silly goats in front of the television cameras. This was my first encounter with adversarial government groups and Nader lawyers. The event was just short of a disaster. While our engineers, doctors, and scientists performed in a highly professional manner, the technical information fell on deaf ears. I doubt that we could have done better with other approaches, but as Nader lawyers cross-examined us, it became apparent that they weren't after data, they were trying to destroy the credibility of the Dow Chemical Company by attacking each of our witnesses. They would repeat questions, go back and try to distract us in some manner so as to find a weakness in our answers. The whole thing was a kangaroo court. Boy, that was a stunner to me.

"When I returned to Midland I went over to Pruitt's home, because he had been ill. I didn't know Mac Pruitt very well at that time. He had just come up from Texas to head up all Dow research. I told him about our experience in Washington and what a godawful thing he had sent me to do. I told him I didn't like it one bit and that I didn't want to do anything like that again in my whole life. Pruitt got out of bed and said, 'Gee, Etcyl, I was going to offer this to you as a full-time job. Because of our product lines and our technical strength, we're going to be involved in this type of activity for a long time. Do you mean you're going to turn me down?' I hadn't turned down too many jobs at Dow, so I thought, 'Well, he's the top person in Dow research; I'd better be listening'. I said, 'Okay, I'll do it, but I haven't the foggiest notion of what we're headed into'."

"I've had brilliant breaks at Dow", he said. "This new job at Dow brought me into an absolutely astounding world. I eventually became a vice president (in 1978) and was put in charge of toxicology, medical, and regulatory matters. I was asked to organize the company so that it would be in a better position to deal with the issues that would be coming to it from OSHA, EPA, TSCA, NIOSH, etc. I asked V. K. Rowe, the greatest toxicologist that Dow had, to leave the tox lab and come on my staff, to be my brains and to be a spokesman on matters relating to toxicology. I set about organizing the company to deal with all types of adversarial attacks and made certain that we had the proper technical information to answer the many questions that would be asked of us. We developed computer programs for the tox information on all Dow products and made them available to Dow operations around the world. We formed product management teams to manage our technical base and to react quickly to outside groups challenging our products. I became very involved in trade associations, headed up study groups, took people all over the world, fought battles everywhere. I helped to get the CIIT (Chemical Industry Institute of Technology) launched and served as advisor to a number of university groups and to the ACS. It was all very exciting, but very demanding".

"I had a lot of doubts when I went into it", Blair said. "It takes a lot out of you. You have to be able to take it. There's a lot of raw meat involved when you get involved in issues such as dioxins, carcinogens, mutagens, teratogens..."

These issues were international in nature, and his duties carried Blair all over the world in the next dozen or so years. "My life at Dow was just one fantastic series of events after another", he said. "In looking back, I am now amazed at what all I did experience, from walking with Anwar Sadat in Cairo after his return from Israel, to scientific discussions in the burnt-out Reichstag building in Berlin, to discussing regulatory matters with Sen. Albert Gore of Tennessee. Each day was a challenge and a new adventure. I always wanted to get up and get at it".

During his last year at Dow before retiring, he received the Public Affairs Award from Region Five of the EPA for contributions to science and public policy, an exceptional honor because the organization very seldom honors industrial figures. "I knew Douglas Costle (administrator of EPA in the middle'90's) and many of his people at EPA, but I certainly would not classify the two of us as the best of friends", Blair said. "While we respected each other, we had many differences. I always tried to stand on the facts. I had developed a strong working relationship with one of Costle's key administrators, Stephen Jellinek, the head of TSCA (Toxic Substances Control Act). I had become acquainted with him through the CMA (Chemical Manufacturers' Association). This was during the Carter Administration, not one of the best times for us. I was chairman of the CMA committee responsible for industry input to EPA during the formation of TSCA. Frequently I met with Jellinek to present industry's views on certain TSCA requirements and over the years had gotten to know him very well. He was also in charge of the EPA registration section for pesticides. We developed such a relationship that whenever a major decision was to be made by EPA, he would call me and let me know in advance. I likewise would inform him of some action by industry so that the agency would not be caught off guard. In a way we were helping each other with our press problems. I once had him visit Midland and speak to our local ACS. I was a firm believer that one should always know one's enemy, because failure to do so could prove disastrous..

"Certain Dow people like David Rooke didn't like that", Blair said. "He didn't want anyone touching bases with anybody in government. One day as he was making plans to fly to Washington to raise cain about something that EPA had done, I received a phone call from Stephen Jellinek. He informed me that the word was out that Mr. Rooke was coming to Washington to blister EPA, and there were other things he told me at the time that I have since forgotten. Rooke had just been put in charge of Dow USA, so he was out to show how things would be done under his command. Jellinek said to me, 'Etcyl, if this thing occurs, we will drop a few bombs on your Mr. Rooke and I can tell you that the press will crucify him. He is the typical Texan coming to Washington to personally handle matters this way, but it just won't work with the federal government. We will have the press there during his talk and they will be primed with lots of questions from our side of the fence.' I knew I had a problem. I had to find a way for Rooke not to make a fool of himself, but I had to handle it rather gingerly. I knew he would be leaving shortly and that he was in conference with his new staff and the business managers that would be reporting to him. I decided I had to go into the meeting room and not send a secretary in to confront him. 'David', I said, 'I have an important piece of information I must get to you and I don't know how to get it to you other than to come in here and give it to you.' He took me to an adjoining room. I said, 'Take it for what you think it's worth, but the top administrator in EPA that deals with our chemicals under TSCA has called and told me that the word is out that a Dow executive is to give a speech in Washington and that he will use certain phraseologies in an attack on EPA. If this happens, it could make a number of current issues under discussion between Dow and EPA most difficult'. Rooke thanked me and left.

"Later a most interesting thing happened. I'd been away on a trip myself, and on returning to my office I found a note on my desk in David Rooke's handwriting. It read, 'Anytime you have an important piece of information for me, come right on in'.

"At times Jellinek and I had our disagreements. I remember a very large meeting in Washington called by EPA to obtain industry input on some proprosed regulations. I had been asked to respond for CMA and Dow. I was about halfway through my presentation when Jellinek informed me that my time was up. I turned and said, 'I will not leave this stage until I have finished. I have come one thousand miles at EPA's request and I will not leave until I have made this presentation, because there are certain points that I specifically want to get across.' I received a huge applause. There must have been a thousand people in the audience. I got more attention at that meeting than anybody else."

Blair retired in 1986 and was succeeded by David T. Buzzelli, but still continued to keep an attentive eye on the relationship between Dow and the federal government. By 1994 he felt the company had gone beyond the point where he felt comfortable with it. "I think; today, that Dow has gone too far with government", he said. "They have tried to kid themselves that if they stay close, government won't hurt them. You can't get that close to government. You don't ever want to get that close, because by nature government will always be examined by others, the environmentalists and the news media, and they will make mincemeat out of you. You need to be close enough to know what is going on from a professional point of view, but not so close that you are viewed as influence peddling. Play your role, be involved, but don't ever think they're going to do you a favor..... I believe Dow went too far, years ago, when we wanted to fight government over every issue...you have to learn how to play the game from year to year. It's just like politics; it's always changing.

"I don't know that there is a hard set of rules. In the first place, you do need good information to make good decisions. The basic reason to have the information is so that you can make a proper decision, not to convince somebody else. You must have that, otherwise you lose your associates and your friends. You know how to do the right thing, that is what your mommies and daddies taught you to do. Then you have to become politically astute....Ask yourself the question, 'If I do that, what happens?' and 'If I don't do that, what happens?', and then make your decision. There's often too much of 'We're going to do it my way', and maybe to a degree the policy was 'We're big and we're an aggressive company; we can do what we want to do'."

Nonetheless, Dow's top management, he said, always had his respect and admiration. "Ben Branch was a great leader", he said. "He did not like to be the spokesman, but he was committed to safety and doing the right thing. I remember when we were conducting the analytical studies for Reserve Mining. Our analytical labs were measuring the fiber size and amount of asbestos that Reserve Mining was releasing into Lake Superior. Lo and behold, someone in the company sent samples of the waste water from our chlorine cells to the analytical laboratory for analysis. We had substantially higher amounts of asbestos in our waste water than Reserve Mining had in their discharges. You can imagine what this would do to our visibility, on top of napalm and Agent Orange. I showed the results to Pruitt. He said, 'We have to go higher with this', so we went to Barnes (Earle B. Barnes, then president of Dow USA). Barnes said, 'This is a bigger issue than I can handle by myself'. He requested that we get Levi Leathers (Dow V.P., Manufacturing) and meet him in Ben Branch's office. (Branch was then president and CEO of Dow.) I took Jessie Norris (of Dow's Chemical Biology Research group) with me, to explain the toxicological significance of the findings.

"We explained everything to Branch. He turned to Levi and said, 'How long will it take you to get those fibers down?' Levi said, 'Oh, probably six to eight months'. Branch said, 'I want it down in three months, and if anybody is injured or if these people come back in here and tell me we've got a problem, I'll shut your chlorine production down all over the world', and he got up and walked out. That was commitment to product stewardship. That was absolutely superb leadership. And the whole chlorine business changed as a result of that meeting. A totally different process was developed."

One of the things he was most proud of was the establishment of the Chemical Industry Institute of Technology. "This was an outstanding industry achievement and I wish there were more", he said. "I give all the credit to Mac Pruitt. Mac Pruitt couldn't spell toxicology when we started out on this adventure, but he became its greatest supporter. Mac was a good lisstener and a great learner. I'm certain that when Earle Barnes brought him here from Texas, they hadn't thought much about toxicology and hadn't paid much attention to toxicity. When the cancer problem associated with vinyl chloride hit the press, things began to happen. Pruitt became very concerned about other commodity chemicals. 'Why should Dow invest millions of dollars for vinyl chloride toxicity studies when every Tom, Dick and Harry can make it?' he said. 'We've got to find a way to pool our resources if we as an industry are ever to get on top of these problems.' So he became the champion and spokesman for CIIT and I became his pair of hands. He and I travelled many miles together in getting industry support. He was a tremendous salesman in pushing this concept. Once he learned something and locked in on it, I'll tell you, he could move mountains. I've seen him shut down the top people in the company, saying, 'We're going to do it our way, we're going to develop this information', etc. He, to me, was one of the truly great Dow leaders.

"Today CIIT has a membership of 50 companies. When we started out there were seven of us, later 13. We at Dow had just completed building our new toxicology laboratory to handle the problems associated with vinyl chloride and the OSHA carcinogens when Pruitt called me to his office and asked what other chemicals might have toxicity problems. I did a fast survey and gave him the results. 'We don't have the wherewithal to handle all the problems coming down the track', I said. We were the world's largest producer of chlorinated and brominated chemicals and they were the suspect chemicals on everyone's list of problems. You name it, we made it. I told Mac, 'We must double the size of our tox lab, but still we will not be able to do all that needs to be done'. Mac told me to go build the lab. There was never an argument. At our first planning meeting in Midland, when our new lab was about half completed, some of the companies interested in forming a CIIT wondered if the idea of a CIIT was just a way of Dow paying for their new lab. It wasn't that at all. Mac wanted an independent institute, completely separate from industry. Industry would run it at the board level and would deal with money matters and management only. The institute would have its own president and an independent staff of scientists.

"Mac Pruitt put the whole thing together. I'll never forget the time we were in the Dupont boardroom where the Dupont people were giving Mac a hard time. They didn't need a CIIT, they said; they had their own laboratories. Mac knew how to make decisions, and he knew how to force decisions. We had been discussing the need for a CIIT for some time with ten company men seated around the table, when suddenly Mac stood up and said, 'Well, I have a plane to catch in 30 minutes, and when I leave here, we're going to build CIIT'. He walked over to Monte Throdahl of Monsanto and asked, 'Are you with me, Monte?' Monte said 'Yes'. He then proceeded around the table, getting commitments from each, and when he came to the Dupont representative, he walked right by the man and to the next person sitting beside him and asked if he was joining. All of a sudden the Dupont representative jumped up and said, 'Aren't you going to include us?' We knew then that we had them locked up. Mac was a master at doing that kind of thing. And Dupont became very committed to CIIT. CIIT today is a very large research institute located at Research Triangle Park in North Carolina. It employs about 120 scientists.

"Over the years", Blair said, "programs have changed. Early concerns were with cancer. Today the concerns are reproductive problems, genetics, and mutagens. CIIT has been a great success. I think there should be more institutes formed where industry creates scientific organizations to solve society's problems instead of leaving everything to the government."

Today, at age 84, Blair is still an occasional public speaker and more frequently a world traveller. In his basement he has a collection of several thousand CDs, all of them recordings of classical music. He is still devoted to a dozen or so professional organizations as well. In between these activities and his children and grandchildren, he manages to enjoy life to the full.

Raymond Rigterink

Chapter 9

Two-a-day Ray

Ray Rigterink had an extraordinary talent. He was a "synthesis" chemist. Give him a chemical formula -- pesticides are invariably terribly complex molecules -- and he would quickly figure out how to make it.

In the pesticides world, half the battle is figuring out the easiest (and thus cheapest and best) way to formulate a pesticide that has been found to have an effect on one or more of the pests that devour and destroy the world's crops. When the researchers turn up a chemical that is effective against the pests they then have to figure out how to make it in quantity for sales purposes, and that was where Ray came in.

One day early in his career Ray solved one such complex chemical problem in the morning, and a second one in the afternoon. Such speed and facility was unheard of with the rather rudimentary lab equipment available in the 1940's, and from then on he was known as "Two-a-day Ray" to his colleagues and his fame as a synthesizer spread rapidly within the company and as time went by , in the industry.

Western Michigan, where he came from, is heavily populated by immigrants from the Netherlands, and Ray was born into one such Dutch family on a farm a dozen miles from Holland, Michigan, in 1916. After his early education in a country schoolhouse and at the Holland High School he enrolled at small Hope College in Holland as a chemistry student, emulating an uncle who was a chemist and following in the footsteps of an older brother.

Hope's entire chemistry faculty consisted of two professors, and its lab equipment could generously be called antiquated, but Rigterink managed to earn an assistantship at Purdue when he graduated and went on to acquire a master's degree in organic chemistry at Purdue in 1941.

"I was just an average student, really", 'Ray said, "and I never had any idea of doing research", but there's where he landed. When Dow's recruiting chief, Steve Starks, made him a job offer he snapped it up and went to work for the company in February 1941, a few months before Pearl Harbor. There he found himself assigned to "Lab 10" of Dow's Organics Laboratory, working for Dr. Ralph P. Perkins. 1

Perkins, he said, "always wanted to boss somebody else", so "he wasn't very well liked, really".

As a single man arriving in Midland his main problem was finding a place to live. Midland and Dow were already heavily involved in the war effort, and housing was at a premium. He finally rented a family's spare room, but that still left the problem of food. "There weren't many places to eat in town", Ray said. "There were only three or four restaurants. The only one I can think of is the Frolic Sweet Shoppe on Main Street. Winifred Cox ran that place -- and that was closed on Sunday. On Sunday we usually went to a place on Saginaw Road, La Bree's. Then there was a sandwich shop downtown. Those were about the only places to eat in town."

"At that time the Presbyterian Church had a dinner for single people in town once a month", he said, "and that was about the only good meal we got in the whole month".

At one of those church meals he met a young lady named Leta who taught at the Carpenter Street School. "We got married in 1944", he said.

In the Organics Lab they put him to work immediately working on catalysts to make butadiene from butene. It turned out to be a key wartime project. The Japanese had followed up on their Pearl Harbor attack by capturing the rubber-making areas of the Far Pacific, cutting off the principal rubber sources of the U.S. in the Far East. A substitute for that rubber immediately became vital to the war effort, and that substitute became SBR -- Styrene-Butadiene Rubber.

"We developed the Type B Catalyst for making butadiene", Ray said. "It was made over in Ludington (Mich.)".

Once the war started, life for young men of his age bracket was dominated by the possibility of being drafted into the armed services. "I always got classified 1-A in the war (meaning subject to immediate draft) and they (Dow) always had to appeal in order to get me back, because I was working on butadiene, you know. I think there were only three people in Dow who were younger than me who got deferments. I certainly wouldn't have gotten one without the company asking for it."

Many of the compounds he developed went on the K-list, a list of compounds that the company knew how to make and had actually made, but for which there was at the time it was made no known use. A sample of the compound was kept, along with data on what was known about it. The K-list over time grew to include thousands of chemical compounds and became one of the Dow company's most valuable research properties. It has provided the starting point for many of the research successes the company has enjoyed. 2

At the end of World War II the agricultural chemicals research function at Dow was reorganized, with Etcyl Blair in charge, and Rigterink was assigned to this group. Blair was working in the phosphorus field, organic phosphorus chemistry, and Ray was given the job of working with heterocylcic compounds and organic phosphorus compounds. 3

"One scientist made most of our products", Blair said, "a chemist named Ray Rigterink. Ray Rigterink is the kind of person that many would pass over. In fact, he was given to me because some said that he was of no value to the company, he just made compounds. Ray was the kind of scientist who never said a word all day long. He was always working. He made one compound every day. Before he'd go home at night, he'd set up his apparatus for the next day. He'd go to Beilstein, he would work out his formulas, get all of his equipment and chemicals, and the next day he would run his reactions. 4

"One day Ray made a heterocyclic phenol that he could not esterify with phosphorus intermediates, so he sent it to Ag for testing. Lo and behold, it became Coyden, the greatest coccidiostat that Dow ever marketed. The company made millions of dollars from that discovery. I believe that there are certain people who are intuitive and every creative, and if you just leave them alone, they will do wonders for you. Ray Rigterink is just such an individual, the most unassuming guy you'd ever meet in your life. All of our successes in the phosphorus program were due to that one chemist."

Another of Ray's compounds became Zytron, a herbicide that killed crabgrass. "The problem with Zytron was that we took it to market about the same time that Dacthal came onto the market", Blair said. "I can't remember which company made Dacthal, but it was cheaper than Zytron and it was just as effective for the control of crabgrass. It's still used. Zytron was a technical success but a business failure." 5

"It was about this time that Ray synthesized Dursban. However, in those early days many of the business types at Ag just could not see a use for Dursban. So when Ray made Dursban, many at Ag weren't all that interested. Gene Kenaga, however, was very excited about it, and I smuggled some to him for testing. Dursban, of course, became the world's largest-selling insecticide.

"Ruelene was a great animal systemic insecticide made from 2-chloro-4-tertiarybutylphenol. It too was made by Ray Rigertink. Ruelene was a superior product because you need only to pour it on the animal. This made application much easier. The tertiary-butyl part of the phenol molecule made the insecticide fat soluble, so that it would translocate through the skin and back of the animal and kill the larva. Ranchers could run their animals into a slurry of water with the Ruelene suspended in it. A lot of Ruelene was sold in South America and Australia for just such uses."

At the time he invented Dursban, Rigterink said, "I was working on combining pyridinol and organic phosphorus compounds, and I went to a company conference in Seal Beach,
California. It was a conference where we discussed what we were doing, gave speeches, and so on. I talked to Howard Johnston because he was working on chlorinated pyridinols for herbicides, and I told him that anything he had, we would be interested in making organic phosphorus compounds with it. At that time all the organic phosphorus work was done in Etcyl Blair's lab. They didn't want people anywhere in the company working on organic phosphorus compounds because of the toxicity problems and the odor problems. Howard Johnston sent me a sample of the 3,5,6-trichloro-2-pyridinol and I made an organic phosphorus compound out of it. That went on the K-list, and Gene Kenaga found the activity; he was the first one who found the activity of

it. It became the world's largest selling insecticide, but, said Ray, "it took a long time to get to that point. It didn't become that until after the patent ran out".

He remembered going on field trips to see how Dursban was doing against various pests. "I remember going south of Ann Arbor; they had a field test out there, and we went down there. We were real disappointed in the test there. It was a poor year for corn rootworm, and they couldn't find any corn rootworm in the blank one (i.e., field to which Dursban had not been applied). A year or two later we went to Nebraska, and they had a field test down there. The supervisor there was completely sold on Dursban. "He said to us, "What are you guys looking for? This is as good as it's going to get.""

Ray worked in the Dow Organics Lab as a synthesis specialist for 41 years. In 1962 he was promoted to senior research chemist, in 1968 to associate scientist, in 1972 to research scientist. He was awarded the H. H. Dow Gold Medal, the company's highest award for a researcher, in 1979. Along the way he collected 53 U.S. patents and wrote 10 scientific publications on the synthesis of organic compounds, made mainly for the discovery of new commercial insecticides, anticoccidials, anthelmintics, or other pesticides.

He retired at age 66. "I was having trouble with ulcerative colitis and ended up having a major operation and lost my colon at age 70", he said. Seventeen years after his retirement he was one of the seven members of the Dow pyridine chemistry team (including Etcyl Blair and Howard Johnston) who were awarded the "Heroes of Chemistry" award by the American Chemical Society, at its annual meeting that year in New Orleans.

"It's people like Ray Rigterink who make a company great", Etcyl Blair said. "You know, it takes a lifetime to produce a great product and it takes a lifetime to find a great scientist and employee. If you're patient enough, though, and awfully lucky, you'll find a Ray Rigterink".

Chapter 10 -- Sidebar

(Two-a-day Ray)

Ode to a Chemist

There was a chemist named "Ray"
Who never went in for horseplay
He turned the crank
With never a prank
And out came two compounds a day.

Now his lab coat is clean
And his test tubes they gleam
Yet he works at the bench
Despite all the stench
And turns out two compounds a day.

And there's never a tar
That he throws in his waste jar
Because he has the touch
To make things such
Turn into two compounds a day.

With never a cry for more pay
Nor trouble to say even "Hey"
He toils and boils
And works on the spoils
To turn out two compounds a day.

He dips his tie in the pot
Till it reaches the catalytic spot
And now you know that the secret of his success
Is to keep his head out of the mess
While he turns out two compounds a day.

You'll find there's plenty of hay
Says this chemist named Ray
If you show your mettle

Push hard on the pedal
And turn out two compounds a day.

After his long stay
He's found there's a way
To wear a white shirt
Avoid all the dirt
And turn out two compounds a day.

Hence it gives us great pleasure
To present you this treasure
For after working fifteen years
You can see it appears
No trick at all to get two compounds a day.

(Poem written by Charles "Charlie" Villars of the Organics Laboratory,
The Dow Chemical Company, Midland, Michigan, c. 1956, occasion not
recalled. Courtesy of Etcyl H. Blair, Midland)

Paul Ludwig

Chapter 10

Life at the Double Lazy V

As a farm boy in central Ohio, Paul Ludwig was totally fascinated by spiders. He spent much of his free time observing them. "They have an extra pair of legs", he said. "They really do. They are really, really fantastic. There are many kinds, many colors, many sizes. And they have many forms of webs. You can look at a web and you know what classification of spider it is".

Encouraged to follow this boyhood interest by Boyd Young, his biology teacher at the Springfield (Ohio) high school, he went on to major in zoology, chemistry, and entomology, first at the University of Ohio at Athens, and then at Wittenberg College, from which he graduated in 1950. He acquired a master's degree, and finally a Ph.D., both in entomology, at Ohio State University. At both Wittenberg and Ohio State he worked on the school's insect collections, making sure they were properly preserved.

His academic career was broken up by a five-year stint in the U.S. Navy during World War II. For most of those years he was a meteorologist in the Pacific theater. Then he came back to Wittenberg and married Ellen Scott, a fellow student whom he met in the registration line.

 His first job out of school was at the Boyce Thompson Institute for Plant Research in Yonkers, N. Y. , where he worked on a research grant from the Ethyl Corporation,   looking for new insecticides. When the grant ran out he looked for a new job, and at an entomology society meeting in Houston he ran into an old friend from Ohio State, Fred W. Fletcher, who was then working in the Agricultural Research department at Dow Chemical in Midland, Michigan.1   Fletcher and Gene Kenaga, who was also at the meeting, told him they had an opening for an entomologist at Dow and invited him to apply for it.

He did, and it was the dawn of a 31-year career as a Dow entomologist.

He flew from New York to Midland to be interviewed for the position. "Somewhere over Cleveland we ran across a weather front that was horrible", he said. "The food was all over the cabin and all over the people. And those that didn't have food all over them, they were sick. I got off in Cleveland and I rode from Cleveland to Midland on a bus, to get there to start my introduction to all of these people. I had no sleep, no change of clothes. It was unbelievable that they ever hired me."2

His first assignment was to reorganize the company's screening tests for potential insecticides. "We would screen the proposed compound against a number of insects", he said. "We'd spray the insects with it and dip them in it, and all this sort of thing, maybe it was a dozen different insects. And then we'd look at the results".

The chemists at Dow would come up with a formulation for an insecticide, and his group was then assigned to screen it. "I used to say to Etcyl Blair that his group made them, and we tested them", he said. "After we'd get a group of them -- insects and chemicals -- together, we could start to make patterns out of it. We could structure different things to make something that kills spider mites or something that kills flies".

In 1962 he was sent down to Texas to serve as head of agricultural research at Dow's Texas Division, succeeding Dr. Robert W. Colby, an animal nutritionist who had established an agricultural chemical research center there in 1953. 3

The center was out at Lake Jackson, a few miles from Freeport. "There were some old ponds there that were part of a river system, and they blocked it off and made a big lake out of it. Lake Jackson was the name of the lake and of the town also. It was very small. Brazoria county contains 1,501 square miles, and 500 of those square miles have an average elevation of six inches above mean tide. Shrimp and mosquitoes were abundant".

"Oh, Lordy, did we have mosquitoes", he said. "I wound up as chairman of the board of mosquito control for the county. We had so many, we had all the people signed up for mosquito control. This is the truth, I'm not lying, but cattle that grazed out there in some of those areas, there were so many mosquitoes that they would inhale them and their nasal passages would get stopped up with mosquitoes. We would do what we called a mosquito count. You'd face into the wind and count the number of mosquitoes from your waist to your cuffs. You'd wear a pair of light-colored pants and then you could count the number of mosquitoes. After a while, we couldn't count them. We just estimated. It was tough. Lake Jackson was one of the first places to legally set up mosquito control.

"We sprayed, primarily using malathion. Have you ever seen the fog where they belch copious smoke out of the exhaust and that carries the insecticide particles that contact and kill the mosquitoes? That was us."

"Sometimes we made headway and sometimes we didn't, but the thing is, mosquitoes are lazy", he said. "They'll go with the wind. They won't fly upwind, but they'll fly downwind. That's what you have to remember. Mosquitoes just fly and rest, fly and rest. So if you make contact with them where the area is treated, they would die. But they'd move into Lake Jackson, the city, and people were unhappy. In the end we got it pretty well under control. We did it with the plane and the foggers around the cities and we did a lot of work along roadside ditches, treating them with pesticides".

The first research product he worked on at Lake Jackson was Lorsban, a new insecticide designed especially for cotton and corn growers. "It was then called K-7505", Paul said. "We remembered them all by the K numbers -- they got commercial names later. Another that became commercial was K-26015, which was Ruelene. Ruelene was a systemic phosphate that we could put on cattle, for example, that would take care of all the insects that were internal in the animals, the main ones being the cattle grub and the heel fly".

"That's a pretty big potential business because you've got so many millions of cattle in the United States. The economic loss occurs primarily in the latter part of the insect's life. The heel fly deposits its eggs on the legs of the animal as it moves around the pastureland, and the cow licks the eggs and swallows them and the egg gets into the body. When the eggs are hatched they start a small journey, migrating through the tissues of the animal and locating in one of two locations --- either along the spinal column or in the esophagus tissue in the gullet. One species migrates to the back area, causing a big boil full of purulent material with a larva on the inside. They digest a hole through the hide and in that way get oxygen to breathe, but what they do in this process is to destroy the prime hide, along with the tissue along the backline of the cattle."

The system Dow was developing called for a liquid to be poured over the animal's back, killing the larvae and interrupting the insect's life cycle.

"We did have Ronnel", Ludwig said. "That was the early one, and we did develop that. It involved a big bolus which was about three inches long and about as big around as your thumb, and we had to take a bolus gun and place it it in the animal's throat. So it wasn't easy to administer. That was the first really systemic insecticide for cattle. And it was good for fleas, flies, and a vast array of other insects".

The Lake Jackson laboratories raised their own insects for use in their experiments. "We raised the insects in the lab, and we'd knock them out with carbon dioxide", Ludwig said. You could take CO2 and anesthetize them, and then you could count them out. You could just sort out the number you needed and place them in a container. We would spray the insect larvae or pour the material over them. Then we would go back 24 hours later and count the live and the dead larvae. That's the secret. You had to be able to count to a hundred. If you couldn't, you didn't make it".

"We would do replications of various tests. At one time, I don't remember the exact number, but I think it was 60 or 70 different insects that we reared for testing. We put the data in the computer early on. I'd have to do all that -- tally it all up and get it to the research group at the computers, and they'd enter the data on the computers".

The Lake Jackson labs, which employed, he said, about 15 senior scientists and 20 researchers at that period, also had its own cattle ranch for large-scale testing of its products. "We had cowboys on the staff and we even had one cowgirl", he said. "She was the daughter of one of the cowboys."

Dow had extensive holdings of land around the Lake Jackson area, he said, and "we ran cows on about 5,000 acres of it. We also had a cattle ranch about 20 miles down the Texas coast at Matagorda, and we had 300 or 400 animals there too". The herd was run as a regular commercial cattle operation, and the testing was incidental.

"We had bulls and heifers, and they'd have calves and the next year we'd sell the calves", he said. "We had a regular registered brand that we used on the cattle, the Double Lazy V. It was patterned after the Dow company logo, the Dow diamond, split into two V's. They were 'lazy' because they were lying on their sides".

The primary commercial herd at the Double Lazy V ranch consisted of eighty head of registered Brangus, he said, a Brangus being a mixture of Brahman and Aberdeen Angus. Brahman cattle tolerate the heat, he said, and insects and ticks love them, and "that's why we had them, but they are nasty. I mean, they're not nice. They're just not nice. Good cows, but bad-tempered".

Once a bus-load of securities analysts, "all dressed up in coats and ties", came to visit the research station , and Ludwig and his crew showed them around and ran some cattle into a v-shaped chute, narrow at the bottom and wider up top, "so we would walk along the cattle walk up top and rub our hands over their backs or whatever we wanted to do with them. We loaded the chute with cattle, and the first one in went over the top and side of the chute and scattered the analysts in every direction. None of them were hurt but they got right back on the bus and left. After that we made sure we always had some tame ones around in case of visitors".

Ludwig also led the Dow company into the catfish business. "We have a reservoir of 1,800 acres on Dow property down there in Texas", he said. "It was made by going around with a bulldozer and throwing up a levee, and then they filled this big thing with water. It was just a great place to grow fish, and the thought occurred to me, 'Why not grow fish in this place on purpose, and sell them?' So we decided we were going to raise catfish there. We built big floating traps and we put little fingerlings in there, small ones. And we provided them with food. We hoped with the food that was supplied to them and the food naturally coming through, that they would eat it and grow. So we stocked these tanks, which had quarter-inch openings, with big trap doors on top. We began to raise fish, and everything was fine, and we built some ponds where we could do research on raising fish."

The project attracted a lot of attention immediately, getting national press attention, and from that "a lot of other people got the same idea at the same time". Suddenly catfish ponds were springing up everywhere. Nevertheless Dow stayed in the catfish business for four or five years, and then, Ludwig said, it got to the point where "a lot of the local people started putting ponds out and doing it. They had tanks to hold the food, and then you blow it out on these ponds. It worked pretty well". The catfish would convert about two pounds of feed into one pound of fish, he said, "so there was money in it".

That was the start of the catfish industry. "You go to the fish market today and you will find pond-raised fish for sale", he said. But, as it has in many other cases, Dow decided it was in the business of making and selling chemicals, not catfish, and it left the catfish business to others.

Undismayed, Ludwig turned his attention to another foodstuff -- the shrimp that were so plentiful in the Freeport area, still today an important shrimping port. Why not raise shrimp as a commercial proposition, he wondered.

"We started out with aquariums, small ones, in the laboratory, and we just built shelves like bookshelves and we put aquariums all over them. We put shrimp in there, and the first thing we found out is that shrimp don't like each other. They've got a big rostrum that comes out of their heads, a pointed bony structure, and they ram the other shrimp in the tank with it, and actually wound the other shrimp, and you would wind up with one shrimp in the tank. So everything we had to rear, we reared in individual containers. But we were able to do that. We were able to go out into the ocean, put the nets down, and collect what are called 'gravid' females. These shrimp have clusters of eggs on their abdomens. We would bring them in and put them in the saltwater they normally exist in, and then we'd raise the temperature very slowly. At a certain time they'll release all those eggs, and that way we got these tiny little larval shrimp. They're just like floating detritus on top of the water surface. But every one of those little specks was a live shrimp. In about 180 to 200 days we could get a shrimp sized for market. Shrimp bring quite good money. We had a project in conjunction with Texas A&M, and they had some ponds located with us on the marsh. That was a big, big venture. We raised a lot of shrimp".

The shrimp business lasted about three years, he said, and then "we got flooded out. We had hurricanes come through that flooded us out".

In spite of all these other projects, he said, "the big thing that drove our work was coccidium control. This is a very small organism that gets into the crop and digestive system of chickens and other fowl and causes a disease, coccidiosis. So we added certain compounds to the diets of chickens to test their biochemical activity against these organisms. From the first day the chick was born they started getting a special diet. They had regular food, but it contained a small amount of the test compound."

The first really successful coccidiostat was a chemical called zoalene, developed by Dr. Theo A. Hymas of Dow. (Chicken feed with zoalene in it was called "zoamix"). "At one time we had probably 90 or 95 per cent of the medicated poultry diet", he said, "but every time we would get ready to release a new one, Merck would come out with another one that was better".

For years the two companies competed to develop the best coccidiostat, with Merck the eventual winner. "Merck had amprolium",4 Ludwig said. "They came out with a coccidiostat that was about, as I remember the data, a fourth of the dose that we were giving the birds. It was very good, and they took the major part of the business".

In 1974 he left Texas and Lake Jackson and transferred back to Midland with a totally different assignment -- to computerize the agricultural chemical business of Dow. "I came back to Midland and I had a lot of fun, for me", he said. "We got into computers. We had got computers early and all of the insect data was computerized. It was laboriously sorted with the old punch-key system, but then we started to get modern computers, and I got involved with that. They gave me one of the top guys from the Dow computer lab, Walter L. (Les) Berry, and he and I worked together for about a year and a half. We got the Dow ag department computerized".

"I had some interesting experiences with that", he said. "It used to be that we'd sit around the table and discuss projects and report on the things we were going to do. You'd come up with a project, and for two or three days we'd argue about whether we were going to get the $3,000 or so that you needed to spend on the project. Along came the computer, and they asked me, 'How much money do you need?' I did some talking and buzzing around, and I said, 'I need $3 million'. And they said, 'Okay'. For $3,000 we'd argue about it, but for $3 million we'd never talk. We started it and it worked out pretty nice. I got to visit all of the research laboratories and field stations, so I was fortunate to get involved in that."

"I got to be pretty knowledgeable about computer work. I even got to where we could take and analyze the data and decide what we wanted to do. We could have all the plants we had growing and we could tell which bugs were going to be chewing on the different ones because of this batch of stuff. If things were such that you wanted to look for something that was specific, you could do that. Tordon was one of them. We did a lot of the early, early computer stuff with Tordon. We computerized all of the ag department, and then we started overseas. Eventually we were all tied together via computers all over the world. If somebody was working on one product and I was working on another, we could compare notes on what we were doing. One of the things we ended up with was a program that we could run through and tell you how much you could use for this product on such and such a problem. It was early work, but at that time it was the leading art".

In the twilight of his career he became a recruiter for the company and was responsible for Dow recruiting in Michigan, Ohio, Indiana, and Kentucky. "My responsibility was to get to know the staff in the science departments of schools in those states. They would test our products along with others, and we would get all of the data back, so it was a good program".

"Then my wife Ellen got a brain tumor and I had to quit traveling", he said. He retired from the company in 1986 and became a care-giver. "She died on September 8, 1988", he said. The Ludwigs had had four children of their own, and had adopted two Korean girls and two Latin American boys in addition.

"My wife read quite a bit", he said. "She read a book called 'The Seed from the East', about the orphans from China5, and got it in her mind that she was going to adopt some. We found out that Korea is probably a little easier than China, so we made out an application and went through all of the process. We paid money for the baby and she went to Korea to get the baby. With the second one, I didn't want to be deprived of that privilege, so I went to Korea myself and got the second baby and brought her home.

"And then we became a foster home. We had some 40 children, and some of them never left. We had a Latin American boy who weighed five pounds and was five weeks old. They told us he wasn't going to live, but my wife decided that that baby was going to live. She fed him with a little eye dropper and gave him just a little bit at a time. She'd get up every hour or two and give him a little bit. He's now a commercial photographer. Then his brother -- they are actual brothers, they had the same mother but not the same father -- was beaten and thrown around from place to place and everything, so we adopted him too, and that gave us eight. And they've all done pretty well".

Throughout all these vicissitudes his fascination with spiders has never flagged. "They fly", he said. "Did you know that spiders fly? They fly on gossamer. They get up on a stick or a point on a rock and they put out voluminous amounts of silk. The wind comes along and picks them up and takes them to who knows where. That's how they spread to different places".

Cleve A. I. Goring

Chapter 11

A Tough Slog

Soil. Dirt. The good earth.

That's where man's food comes from. So an intimate knowledge of the earth is vital to agriculture and food production. And all too few of us have made a serious study of soil and the ways it can be made to yield more food for the hungry millions.

One of those rare birds who have studied the soil is Cleve A. I. Goring, Dow's first soil scientist, who joined the company in 1952 and spent the next 34 years studying the interrelationship of soil and chemicals and the voracious tiny beasties that infest the soil and rob the goodness from it.

Goring was originally a British citizen, born and raised in Georgetown, British Guyana, a British colony. His mother thought he should go into agriculture, "because that was what was in the colonies", and he headed for the agricultural college of McGill University, Macdonald College, in Montreal, Canada, where he studied chemistry and bacteriology. There he won a fellowship which involved going to Iowa State University in the United States. "Going to the states", he said, "that's what I always wanted to do. And I did."1

At Iowa State he acquired master's and Ph.D. degrees in soil microbiology, a wife, and a job as a soil agronomist with the U.S. Department of Agriculture. In the meantime John Kagy, of Dow, out at Seal Beach, California, was looking for a soil scientist. "He basically wanted somebody that knew something about soils because Dow had soil fumigants", Goring said. "The only people he had on his staff were chemists and biologists of one kind or another, but he had no one trained in soil chemistry and microbiology. So he was looking for someone".

Kagy sent Dave Martin, his assistant, to Iowa State as part of this search, and Martin interviewed Goring and offered him the job. California sounded good to both Gorings and they were soon on their way to California. "At that time I was earning $4,300 a year and they offered me

$6,000 a year", he said, "and I had always wanted to go to California ever since I was a little kid. The opportunity came along and we took it".

"Well, I went out there and of course I didn't know anything, absolutely nothing, about industry or the research that was going on there, and I met Kage for the first time, a special kind of guy, I'll tell you, very imaginative and very blunt. I sat down in his office with Dave Martin and him and we talked about this and that. My master's thesis was on the process of nitrification, and my doctoral thesis was on phosphors. But they didn't tell me anything that they wanted me to do, initially. They basically said, 'Well, you know, we're in the soil fumigant business and we'd really like to know how soil fumigants act in soils. We use them for controlling nematodes, but sometimes we get a growth response from them that we don't understand. We'd like you to investigate what is the cause of that. And also, we'd like you to work on the behavior of soil fumigants'. (Kage was the inventor of ethylene dibromide as a Dow soil fumigant). So I said, 'Okay, I'll basically go into the library and do some reading'. Well, I went into the library and I read and I read and I read, and I read and I read. I read for six weeks. Finally Kage said to Dave Martin, 'When the hell is that young man going to get off his kiester and do something?' Dave passed that on to me and I said, 'Well, I guess it's time'.

Goring took on two projects. "The history of soil fumigants indicated that they inhibited nitrification, and that this caused the ammonia nutrition of plants. As a result of that, the plants were stimulated to grow faster. Fumigants do so many things, and in order to untangle whether this was the truth or not, I decided to look for a very specific chemical inhibitor of nitrification. That was one project. The other was that soil fumigants were being applied to soils without any basic understanding of the movement of fumigants through soils, the conditions under which they moved rapidly, slowly, down, so in other words, the fundamental behavior of fumigants in soil was a vast unknown to Dow. That was our second project, to really work out the fundamental aspects of the diffusion of fumigants through soil. That's what I started on, those two projects".

"Dick Youngson, Jack Hemwall, and I made a tremendous amount of progress on the fundamental behavior of fumigants in soils", Goring said. "In the other project, I started screening for nitrification inhibitors. Now, at that time the whole process of screening was not a very efficient

132

process, not for anything. So, in order to be able to screen a lot of chemicals in a short period of time, the whole laboratory, and not just myself, everybody was concentrating on developing tests that could screen large numbers of chemicals rapidly for biological activity. We developed tests that would screen about 10,000 chemicals a year, rapidly. As a result of that, after screening about 30,000 chemicals or so, we discovered this group of chemicals that inhibited nitrification -- the chlorinated pyridines.

"The origin of these chemicals was very interesting. A couple of Oklahoma professors, Brett and Hodnett, decided to explore the chlorination of pyridine rings, especially pyridine, but also methyl pyridines. After they'd done this work, they tested these chemicals in a greenhouse for biological activity, and they found slight herbicidal activity. Well, they didn't have any capabilities for patenting, and they came to Dow and asked Dow to help them get patents on these things, which Dow did. John Spalding was the patent attorney involved. Dow put the chemicals on the K list, and Jim Head of the Organic Research Laboratory, the Britton Lab, did some work on them. A lot of the chemicals that Brett and Hodnett submitted were just mixtures, and Jim Head sort of untangled a lot of these mixtures and put specific chemicals on the K list -- trichloromethyl pyridines of one sort or another. So that's where the chemicals came from. And it turned out that the trichloromethyl pyridines were very good inhibitors of nitrification".

That was the start not only of a new product -- N-Serve, it is called, a nitrogen stabilizer2 -- but of Dow's pioneering work in pyridine chemistry, and Goring was later credited with originating the company's venture into this field. It ultimately resulted in the invention of nine pyridine-based products including N-Serve, and Tordon herbicide.

"We didn't have enough knowledge of pyridine chemistry at that time to make single compounds in high yields", Goring said. "I wanted to test the compounds out in the field so we had to make large quantities of them, and that was a matter of persuading some chemist to come up with a large quantity of the material to test in soil. That chemist turned out to be Howard Johnston, who had been working with us over many years, making chemicals of one sort or another for testing. Howard said, 'Sure, I'll do it', and he did it. The Britton Laboratory was not interested. Ralph Perkins was in charge of the laboratory at that time, and he certainly knew of Jim Head's work. But Ralph basically said, 'You know, we may never sort out how to make those compounds. It's a mess! When you chlorinate methyl pyridine, you just get a big mixture of compounds, and it's a mess'. But Howard went ahead and made us some stuff to go out in the field".

The field work was done by George Turner in California's Coachella Valley, on corn and tomato crops, mixing the new pyridine product with regular ammonium (anhydrous ammonia) fertilizer. "Well, when we put this mixture out on corn", Goring said, "with a huge amount of irrigation water, without the chemical the ammonia converted to nitrate and it was just washed right out of the soil. With the chemical, the ammonia stayed in the surface of the soil and there were huge differences in the growth of this corn. It also turned out that when we put the mixture on tomatoes, the tomatoes, amazingly, showed signs of growth regulator activity. Not only that, if we put the mixture in anhydrous ammonia and put that on tomatoes, it showed tremendous growth regulator activity. These were the observations in the field.".

They decided at this point that they had something. "We put together a little task force and started to figure out what it was in this mixture that was causing these things", Goring said. "Howard Johnston made the pure chemicals, verified their structure and verified the activity. John Hamaker, Carl Redemann, and Dick Meikle were all involved in chromatographic studies in soil, extracting out these chemicals. And that's the origin of N-Serve"

"Of course that didn't solve my problem", Goring said. "I wanted a pure chemical. One day, and I still remember the day, Dick Bailes came down from Pittsburg (California, headquarters of Dow's Western Division) and he said, 'Cleve, I think I've got your problem solved. We were just digging around under certain conditions with this chlorination process and up popped this chemical with 95 to 99 per cent yield', and that was N-Serve. And Howard Johnston and Bill Taplin have just discovered a process for making N-Serve. He said, 'Do you think this will suit your needs?' I said, 'Let me test it'. So I ran through a series of tests on its biological activity and its physical behavior, and I said, 'Perfect! I'll take it'. And then, I think that was the time that we really had the realization that pyridine and methyl pyridines were a raw material that could be chlorinated and manipulated, and by manipulation I mean you can then react those chlorines on the ring with amino groups and hydroxyl groups. You could hydrolyze the chlorine groups. You could do all of the things that you could do with benzene and chlorinated benzene. You could do all of those, and you could make a whole series of chemicals that were analogous to the chemicals derived from benzene that were already on the market. That's really the revelation in the project, that we could do analog synthesis on pyridines, and it was just like benzene. There's only one difference. The biological activity of the pyridine compounds was much greater. That's why all those products came out of that program. And Howard Johnston was the guy that did most of that chemistry. He was a great chemist."

Many years later, in 1983, Goring and Johnston were honored by the American Chemical Society with the "Heroes of Chemistry" award, along with other members of the Dow pyridine team. Johnston had died in the interim, but was not forgotten.3

Tordon, one of the pyridine products, had a problem, Goring said, and that was that it was fairly persistent in soil, and tremendously active on broadleaf crops and weeds. "We recognized immediately that we had to do a lot of work on the behavior of this material in soil", he said, "its rate of degradation, its movement through soil, that sort of thing. To utilize it in agriculture, if you put it on a grass crop, it had to disappear the next year. So we formed a little environmental group. This was in the late 1950's, long before the EPA ever existed, to study the behavior of pesticides in soil. The guys on that group were Dick Youngson, Carl Redemann, Dick Meikle, John Hamaker, who was a great physical chemist, and myself. And we set out to study the environmental behavior of chemicals in soil, and that's how that group got together. Later on we hired Dennis Laskowski, a soil microbiologist, and that group did a tremendous amount of environmental work

"As a result of that I was invited to write and edit a book, by Prof. Douglas McLaren at the University of California, Berkeley. And John Hamaker and I put together that book, the first book, really, on the environmental behavior of organic chemicals in soil." 4

The Seal Beach laboratory, Goring said, was a kind of research jewel for Dow Chemical -- unknown, unsung, but a great producer. "I don't know if you've heard of skunk works in companies", he said, "but that was one of Dow's skunk works. It was a wonderful lab because it had a great spirit. We still have reunions every year. The facilities were terrible -- that's the only way to describe them. It would be totally unacceptable today -- totally. Kage was appreciative of every person he hired, but he was a tough guy, a demanding guy. Sometimes he'd get mad at people and really abuse them, and sometimes he was very understanding. I got along very well with Kage".

Goring in 1964 became assistant director of the laboratory, and in 1969, when Kagy retired, became its director. By that time the outdated old Seal Beach lab had been closed up and the whole operation moved to Walnut Creek, California, the company's main West coast research center.

In 1968 he took a one-year sabbatical from Dow. "That was a period of time when Dow was encouraging its top scientists to take sabbaticals", Goring said. "I don't think that period lasted very long, but Kage said to me, 'Gosh, Cleve, you should really apply for that program. It's a tremendous opportunity'. You were paid your salary -- free, gratis -- your entire salary for a year. I said, 'Gee that sounds like a good thing to me'. So I went home to my darling wife and I said, 'How would you like to go on sabbatical for a year?' She said, 'I'm packing'. That was arranged by Julius Johnson. I had a choice. I could go anywhere in the world that I wanted to go. I considered going to Australia, that was one possibility. I considered going to the University of Wageningen in Holland. That was where a lot of good, fundamental soil fumigation work was being done. And I considered going to Rothamsted in England. Rothamsted is the oldest agricultural experiment station in the world, a very famous station. I decided to go there for two reasons: one, it was England, so we didn't have to deal with a language problem, and secondly, Rothamsted was doing an awful lot of work on N-Serve. They were very interested, so I wrote to the station, and they said, 'Okay, sure, you can come'. So we decided to go to England and Rothamsted".

Adjusting to the British research regime took, he said, a little doing. "I mean, when I arrived at the lab in the morning, there wasn't anybody there. About 10 o'clock or so, they were having tea and lots of discussions. At noon, we would go out to the local pub and have a half-pint and a sandwich. Then we would roll back to the laboratory and do a little bit of work. By mid-afternoon we were ready for tea again. A lot of time was spent talking, but the talk was all about science and experiments and so on. The English are great scientists. They have a reputation for basically talking about science, and then they'll do one key experiment and they may do another key experiment. Whereas Americans, they'll just overwhelm you with work, and then think about what they've done. But that's the English characteristic, and people often don't understand it.

"I remember visiting the University of Reading, and there was a guy from Australia who was there on a sabbatical. When I went to his office, he pulled me inside it and closed the door. The first thing he said to me was, 'Cleve, how do you make the buggers work?' So the English have that easygoing reputation. But they think; that's why they're great scientists. If you look at the history of science, you'll find that there are a tremendous number of Nobel Prize laureates that come from Britain".

When Goring came back to his old job, as assistant director of the lab, after his sabbatical, he found Kagy nearing retirement, and the laboratory in turmoil. "The guys in the laboratory", he said, "one after the other, came into my office and said, 'Cleve, I'm quitting. Kage is going bananas. He just cannot deal with this laboratory any more'. A whole bunch of guys told me, 'We just can't stand it. You've got to do something about it'. So I said, 'Okay, I'll try'. Etcyl Blair had taken over as R&D director for ag, and the next time he came out to California I told him, 'Etcyl, I've got a proposition for you. You know, Kage is having a hard time dealing with his job. Why don't we just switch jobs? You make me director of the laboratory and basically make Kage some sort of senior guru of the laboratory'. Etcyl said, 'Let's do it'. And he did a marvelous job of making that switch. Kage never ever resented it. He was happy that happened. He was put on a special projects deal, and before long he came to me and said, 'Cleve, it isn't fitting and proper that as director, you sit in that little office and I'm in this big office. Let's switch offices'. And we did. He brought his stuff into my office and I took my stuff into his office, and we made the switch just like that. Now, how often does that happen?'"

The dispersion of the Dow company's agricultural activities, with laboratories and production facilities scattered about in Michigan, California, Indiana, Texas, and other places, he said, "has been a curse on the ag business, really", and "when they finally put the whole thing together and made it a global business and moved it down to Indianapolis, that was a wise, wise move."

In 1981 he was appointed to a position as technical director of Dow's agricultural division by M. E. (Mac) Pruitt, then the corporate R & D director. "This technical director had no line authority at all", Goring said. "We had five or six different ag groups around the world because we were pursuing the global expansion of Dow, and behind that was the desire to let the (geographical) areas do their own thing in terms of developing Dow products all around the world. Ag was doing the same thing. My job was to work on research budgets for the world, and I had absolutely no line authority at all. Basically, I was a staff guy for Pruitt. The first time Mac called me in, he said, 'Cleve, you don't think your job has any teeth, but you have my teeth', and I thought to myself, well, those are big teeth. That's alright with me. For a few years I was looking at the entire world ag business and looking at research and the cost of research. It turns out that traditionally Dow's research expenses in heavy chemicals are three or four percent. But the ag business isn't like that. It's more like the pharmaceutical business, not quite as far in that direction, but it just takes more research. As I looked at the actual business, the sales, what was easy to see was that each geographic area was developing the products they were interested in. So the whole development of products and the marketing of them worldwide was pretty fragmented. The only products I can think of in which we really did pursue worldwide development, were two -- chlorpyrifos (Dursban), and Tordon. The thing about it is, that when it comes to being competitive, building a plant, the bigger the plant, the cheaper it costs to make the product. I mean, that's Dow's strength. And here we were, not developing all of the markets around the world for each of our products. We'd develop a market here in the U.S. for this product and then in Europe it was another product that they were pushing, and so on. So it was pretty obvious that from the standpoint of economics, the economics of products, that we should have global development of ag products and a global approach to research and development. That basically was a goal that I pursued.

"I wrote a report on this, and I started it up through the U.S. organization and they said, 'Yep, it makes sense'. But it wasn't until I took that report and laid it on Bob Naegele's desk and said, 'Please, Bob, read this' that I got any action. At that time he was the great guru of ag. The board had put him in charge of the ag business. Well, he read that report and he must have had a lot of input from other places as well, but it wasn't very long after that when we met as a group, 12 of us, called by Bob, that he announced, 'We're going to have a global ag business'. And at that time he appointed Perry Gehring as the R&D director for the ag business, and John Hagaman as the first president of it".

Prior to that, the fragmentation of the ag business caused Dow to sometimes not make very good decisions on the products they were going to develop, he said. "When I say decisions, I mean economic decisions", Goring said. "We had products that from a biological standpoint were very good, but economically, they just didn't make money. There was a very good reason for that. We kept judging these products as to whether or not we should advance them or develop them on the basis of the economic standards of a bulk chemical company, and it just simply didn't work. You have to use different economic standards. That's what it amounted to".

Goring almost automatically became the champion of N-Serve, which he had invented, a product that threatened to die several times. "There weren't very many people at Dow who had any faith in N-Serve", he said. "They didn't. The top of the company was intrigued with it, you know, because what we were selling was something that should go into every pound of ammonium fertilizer, and the fertilizer industry was a big industry. But within our own department, the concept of N-Serve meant nothing to our department. We sold pesticides, you see, and N-Serve was something different. You didn't have research people who knew the product, you didn't have marketing people who knew it, there was hardly anybody in the department that had any kind of background in this potential product, so it was a hard slog trying to develop this kind of interest. They were trying to kill N-Serve, you know. But the product wouldn't die. We just kept plugging along, doing work on it and getting data...

"Before I moved to Midland, I remember, Chet Otis was the manager at that time, and they were having yet another meeting to decide whether to kill the product. I was at this meeting, and they were going over all the various aspects of the product, mostly negative, until John Lillich came along -- Lillich was doing economic evaluation at that time. He ran the economic evaluation on N-Serve, and he told this assembled group that were considering the product, 'Look', he said, 'if we can sell this product, it will make a lot of money'. Of course that didn't convince anybody. The marketers just didn't know how they were going to sell it. They didn't know anything about the market because there was no market. So after the meeting, Chet Otis called me into his office, Chet Otis who had a degree in agronomy, he called me in and he said, 'Cleve, we're going to kill N-Serve'. Well, naturally, I went up in smoke. I told Chet, I said, 'Listen. The Dow Chemical Company has a reputation of being a pioneering company. As far as I'm concerned with N-Serve, we're a bunch of gutless wonders'. I gave him the full blast.

Well, Chet looked at me and he said, 'Okay, Cleve. We'll let it live. Not because I have any faith in it; I don't have any faith in N-Serve. I do have some faith in you'. So I said, 'Okay'.

"Afterwards, Julius Johnson heard what had happened. He said to me, 'Cleve, you're wrong. The Dow Chemical Company is not a bunch of gutless wonders'. I said, 'Okay'. So they let it live, but it's been a tough slog. I understand that it's doing very well this year because the anhydrous ammonia prices have just gone sky high. We are making money on N-Serve. The product survived. Basically, if the world were smart, it would be a much bigger product. But persuading those bohunks in the anhydrous ammonia industry that they need this product that is hard. I have to admit that. It's a tough slog.

"I gave a talk before the marketing department in Midland. I got a standing ovation for this talk, and this talk had to do with N-Serve. I told them, 'N-Serve is like toothpaste. Think about the toothpaste part. Everybody uses toothpaste, and in toothpaste you have fluoride, which basically improves toothpaste. N-Serve is an additive to anhydrous ammonia which makes ammonia a superior product. It's not a stand-alone product. It has to have ammonia'. And they really thought that was a great idea. I told them the introduction of a new product was like crossing the Red Sea. I said, 'You start out on one side, and as you cross that sea you sink deeper and deeper into the red. Your managers are nervous. Everybody up the line is terribly nervous about all this red ink you're accumulating. Finally, at the end of the line you gradually climb out of it and the product becomes profitable and then it starts to grow and become more profitable. And finally, you can forget the Red Sea. I said, 'We're in the Red Sea stage wiith N-Serve right now', and we were. To the everlasting credit of the ag department, when they really decided to launch N-Serve, they gave it the full treatment. Well, maybe not the full treatment. They did sell it. I think the order of magnitude of its sales is now about $30 to $50 million (a year)".

"The intrinsic economics of the product was good", Goring said. "What we had to do was to sell it. But it was a new market. And of course, the other thing that helped it was that it turned out to be an intermediate, an important intermediate for some of the other pyridine products. So, I think it's on its way".

Later in his career, when for a time the Dow Agricultural and Organic Products divisions were joined together, Goring got an entirely different assignment. Bob Hefner, his new boss, said, "I've got a job for you. I would like you to consider being a sort of an outside spokesman for ag. You know, a guy that goes out and fights with the dark forces that are working on the chemical industry". Goring gulped and took on this new job. "He did me a great big favor", Goring said, "because I took on that job and it took me all over the country and all over the world, fighting against those who were attacking ag and the chemical industry. I met a lot of people. I got to know the National Ag Chemicals Association. I served on various research committees at universities and so on, so it really changed the whole kind of job that I was doing. That's how I got into giving a whole bunch of talks. I never really did much public speaking until that happened. It was a good learning experience".

"I gave this talk at Ohio State University and it was on the impact of sustainable agriculture on the ag chemical industry, and this was a hostile audience, quite a few people in it, and this guy got up after I'd given the talk and started asking me some extremely hostile questions. Finally I said to him, 'Look, the ag chemical industry doesn't object to being challenged on the safety and viability of its products, but don't lie about them. Don't tell lies. Make it a scientific discussion'. This guy got up and walked out of the room".

In this battle, Goring said, "Science is winning. Sometimes it's a slow process, but science, in the long run, always wins, I think. Sometimes you don't think it will, but science, in the long run, always wins. That's my view".

He recalled being asked to give a talk to the Dow board of directors on what was coming along in ag chemicals and what was new in the ag chemical business. "Basically", he said, "as part of that talk, I told the board of directors the criteria we were using for new ag chemicals, at least the ones I was promoting. The basic criterion was that the cost of an ag chemical was to be no greater than 20 per cent of the selling price, and that is a totally different criterion than if you were selling chlorine or caustic or some other multi-billion dollar chemical. With them you could have a cost of 50 percent of the selling price and your profits would be great because your research is only about three percent. If every salesman you had out there sold a jillion pounds, not like the ag salesman, where you were lucky to have sales of a million dollars per salesman. So I explained why we had these different criteria, and that our research costs were about 10 per cent, so that when we launched the product, we were sure of its economic success. Dave Rooke (then president of Dow USA) was sitting there and a smile came over his face. 'Cleve, that sounds interesting. It sounds great. But tell me what happened to Bexton?' Now, Bexton was the exact same product as a Monsanto product that they had invented, developed,and were selling on corn. They had a 50-million pound plant to make it and the patents had run out. Dow had a man in process engineering who discovered a new process for this product, a better process and a cheaper process, and he basically sold the idea that we could compete with Monsanto and this product in this market and take a part of it. The only trouble was that Dow put up a 10 million pound plant to make Bexton. Well, you know, you can't compete with a 50 million pound plant with a 10 million pound plant, even though your process is slightly better. So we wound up launching Bexton and it went right off the market because we didn't make any money. So Dave Rooke said to me, 'What about Bexton?' And the only thing I said to him was 'We sinned'. It's as simple as that. Of course, I didn't personally sin. I didn't have anything to do with it, but I took the responsibility for the ag department. And we did sin. Every time we had those projects where, from a biological standpoint it was a beautiful product, like Zectran, or like Bexton, the ones that failed, every time we did that, we sinned. We sinned because we did not apply tough economic criteria to those products".

When he retired, in 1986, Goring and his wife moved to Reno, Nevada, where one of their daughters was located. "Our doctor told us, because my wife had a bad case of asthma in Midland, 'Move to a dry climate', and Reno is a dry climate", he said.

John H. Davidson

Chapter 12

John H. Davidson, plant pathologist

Technically, plant pathologists are specialists in the study and diagnosis of the changes caused by diseases in plants. In lay language they try to figure out how to make plants produce more and better. John Davidson got interested in becoming one because of his father, who was in the produce business -- fresh fruits and vegetables -- in the Chicago area. The family had a summer cottage on Lake Michigan at Shelby, Michigan, in the West Michigan fruit belt, and in the summers young John would often work at a nearby orchard owned by the firm for which his father worked.

These orchards, John said, required a lot of spraying, and he became familiar with the practice. "In those days, we'd get lead arsenate in fifty gallon barrels", he said. "It was a paste, and we'd dig that lead arsenate paste out and dilute it in a bucket and then pour it into the spray tank. I guess this all sort of intrigued me, so I went from there to studying horticulture at Michigan State" (then called Michigan State College of Agriculture and Applied Science).1

This was in 1932, in the depths of the Great Depression. "It was tough going to school", John said. "I had to work most of the time". Mostly he worked in the university's Horticulture Department itself, where the faculty members were doing various kinds of plant research and required help in weeding and grafting and other horticultural things, for which he was paid 35 cents an hour.

That was also where he met Walter C. Dutton, professor of horticulture and expert in the evaluation of pesticides and fungicides for fruit growers. In the summer terms of 1934 and 1935 Dutton was hired by Dow Chemical to help develop a substitute for lead arsenate. While the arsenates that John Davidson was already familiar with killed the bugs nicely, their potential threat to human health was also beginning to be recognized and a substitute for them was being sought by Dow and others.

Dow purchased a piece of fruit-belt property at South Haven, Michigan, which became the company's first field research station for agricultural products, and engaged Dutton to run the place. Dutton went down to

South Haven and took Davidson with him -- still working for 35 cents an hour as a college student but happy to have gainful employment.

At South Haven the two of them, and later others, began working on the dinitro product that Edgar Britton and Lindley Mills had patented in 1928, developing it as a marketable product.2 The company needed answers to many questions surrounding the product before it could be marketed -- on what kind of fruits was it effective? How should it be used, in what kind of carrier? When and how many times should a tree be sprayed, at what intervals, for maximum effectiveness?

After two summers so occupied, Dutton decided to take up Dow's invitation to become a full-time researcher with the company and left the Michigan State staff to join Dow. And again he took Davidson with him. John found himself on the Dow payroll without having applied for a job or having been interviewed by any of the nabobs at Dow. "He (Dutton) just asked me to come along with him, and that seemed to be agreeable to the folks in Midland , so it worked out fine", he said.

Results were not long in coming. The first dinitro product, called Dow Spray Dormant, was introduced by the company in 1937. It was prescribed for dormant use on deciduous fruit trees for the control of over-wintering mites and insects. 3

South Haven was a very economical operation, Davidson said. "We lived in a hotel and we rented a barn out in the country where we kept our trucks and the experimental materials that came down from Midland, so the costs were minimum. There was no office. We used our hotel rooms as offices for the first couple of years. Mostly we were testing materials for their efficiency and whether they'd damage the foliage and the trees". 4

There was no specifically organized ag department in those days (the 1930's) , he said. "There was Joe Cavanagh, who was in charge of insecticide sales, and Dr. E. C. Britton, and Don Irish, who were the main research people, and Sheldon B. (Ted) Heath, who was the head of the Chemical Engineering Laboratory. That's where these things were formulated, and then they'd ship them down to us, where we would evaluate them out in the field. That was kind of the ag department in those days. The formal organization into a department only came along later, at the end of World War II, when Bill Britton kind of put it all together".

Before the war, he said, most of the agricultural products were inorganic chemicals, such as a Dow product brought out in 1938 or 1939 and sold under the name of "App-L-Set". "We discovered that naphthalene acetic acid sprayed on apple trees would stick the apples on the tree in the fall", Davidson said. "This would delay the fruit drop so you got bigger and better apples. We thought we'd try using the naphthalene acetic acid earlier in the season and not have to wait until the end of the season, and in the process of doing that we found that it's a very good material for thinning the fruit.

"Many times", he explained, "too many of the blossoms will set fruit and the fruit's much too thick, but by putting on a little naphthalene acetic acid at a critical time during blossoming, it prevents those blossoms from all setting. So it comes out to be a good material for thinning the fruit, and it's still used today. Or at least a material very similar to it is used. This all started after we happened on this method of thinning the fruit, but it was all just kind of a happenstance. We had plots where we'd use it at different times in the season, and we noticed that when we used it during hlossom time, the fruits set just about right and didn't require any fruit thinning in the summertime. It's kind of a small item, but it's very important to the fruit grower".

World War II was a major watershed for the agricultural chemical business, Davidson said. "During the war, DDT came out and that started the whole era of synthetic, organic insecticides. Before the war it was mostly inorganic chemicals, and then, after the war, the organics took over".

During the war the scope of Dow's farm chemical business expanded rapidly. The company entered the soil fumigant business with a new product, chloropicrin, in 1939, and introduced Dow Selective Weed Killer, another dinitrophenol herbicide, in 1940. In 1942 it established a veterinary research unit in Midland to investigate animal disease control and nutrition. In 1945 it introduced another new dinitro product, calling it Premerge, a weed control agent. By the end of the war, in 1945, Dow had also entered the brand-new DDT field, and was marketing it in formulations ranging from a three per cent dust to a 20 per cent emulsifiable spray.

During this time the company was regularly obtaining deferments from military service for him, but in February, 1943, John said, "I got the feeling that I probably ought to get into the military, so I enlisted. The Navy sent me to Boston for three months and then to small craft training school in Florida for three months, and then I went on a ship in the Mediterranean".

In short order Davidson found himself commanding Patrol Craft 810, a small craft principally doing convoy duty out of Bizerte, Tunisia. "You see, all the convoys would bring in supplies across the Atlantic and all through the Mediterranean. You had to have some kind of convoy. PC810 was equipped like a small destroyer, with a three-inch gun, five fifties, a thirty-five and depth charges and mousetraps up in the bow where you could throw a depth charge off your bow. We had radar and sonar equipment for picking up submarines and radar for picking up planes."

PC810 participated in both the Anzio and Southern France invasions. "We got one submarine", Davidson said. "We were working with a British destroyer and another PC in an area just north of Palermo, Sicily. This was all at night. We sank that submarine, but he surfaced again before we got through. He had one torpedo left and the skipper on the destroyer did a very foolish thing. He turned his searchlight on because he thought that submarine was through. When he put his light on the submarine took aim at it and sank the destroyer with the torpedo he had left".

In all, he spent 18 months in the Mediterranean. At the end of 1945 Lieut. (j.g.) Davidson was mustered out, and returned to South Haven and Dow and the search for a substitute for the arsenates.

"Back in the early thirties people were becoming very concerned with residues on fruits and vegetables, the pesticide residues, and particularly the arsenicals", Davidson said, "because what was being used was mostly lead arsenate and calcium arsenate. These were being sprayed on food crops. As analytical chemistry improved all the time, they were picking up these residues of lead and arsenic on fruits and vegetables. So Dr.

Britton and the people at Dow realized that there was a place for some different types of chemicals for pesticides. They came up with dinitro-ortho-cyclo-hexyl-phenol -- DNOCHP, we used to call it. That was what Walter Dutton worked with when he first came to Dow in 1934 and 1935. At that time it was mostly a dormant spray. We'd use it in petroleum oil as a dormant spray to kill the eggs of aphids, primarily, and some mites and a few other things. Our main target was the codling moth, which was the principal insect pest on apples, and to find a substitute for the lead arsenate that was used on apples. So we were trying to formulate DNOCHP as a good summer insecticide for the control of codling moth. We were never able to do that and keep it safe. But one of the things we did find out was that one of the salts, the dicyclohexamine of DNOCHP, was good for controlling mites.

"We had plots in an apple orchard where we were trying different ways to control the codling moth, and we found one year that the leaves in one plot stayed nice and green, and it was this one salt of DNOCHP, the dicyclohexamine salt, that was controlling the mites, and it did a fair job on the codling moth as well. It was excellent for the control of European red mite. As a result of that work we came up with a product we called DN-111. We sold that for several years for the control of red mite, but it had a real serious problem. If it was used with our mike sulfur or any sulfur product, and it got to be really hot weather, with the sun beating down, it would just burn the apples up, both the foliage and the fruit. So it was limited in its effectiveness. It couldn't be used if there was any sulfur on the tree. Other miticides came along that were better.

"It all went back to Doc Britton wanting to find substitutes for lead arsenate, and the DN materials looked pretty good as an insecticide at first, but later on, they turned out to be good herbicides. The Dow Contact Weed Killer was a DN product, for example."

After his return from military service Davidson continued his work with the phenoxies at South Haven and came up with a product called ColorSet, which improved the apple color development of certain varieties of apples. The active ingredient in this product, which was sold for several years, was 2,4,5-trichlorophenoxypropionic acid. Davidson noticed that in higher doses this compound had a marked herbicidal effect. The result was a herbicide called Silvex, which was more active than the other phenoxy herbicides on some weed species. Dow's product was called Kuron.5

The South Haven field station was closed in 1957 and most of its activities were moved to a 200-acre site known as "the Old Farm" on the outskirts of Midland, a few miles from Dow headquarters, with a 150-acre orchard. "The whole department was getting much larger, and they needed to test new products out in different parts of the world", he said. "Andy Watson went down to Mississippi. Curt Dieter went down to Florida, so they could test on a wider range of crops. And we had these organic herbicides coming along, and the whole area of agricultural chemicals changed, away from fruit and vegetable crops to the more agronomic crops".

Watson established a field station in Greenville, Mississippi, where cotton was the big crop, along with soy beans. In Florida and at Davis, California, it was mainly citrus and grapes. The company soon had a network of stations from coast to coast.

.
In 1972 Davidson's life changed drastically, and he began to spend much of his time in the courtroom rather than in the apple orchard. "Between the misuse of Dow's products and other such problems, and our litigious society, a lot of lawsuits began to come on, and the (Dow) Legal Department didn't know very much about ag chemicals, so they needed a technical adviser to counsel them on these products", he said. "With 2,4-D, for instance, if the user is a little careless, it can do damage outside the area it was intended for. This would come up in court and there would have to be someone who would know something about the product and what the possibilities of careless application were, and that type of thing. That developed into a technical adviser position, and that was my title".

A great many lawsuits came up in the southern U.S., Davidson said, "because they were spraying 2,4-D to control weeds in an adjacent field. "If they were careless in any way, or used the wrong 2,4-D product, there could be a volatility problem and it would affect the cotton. Sometimes this became a very sizable amount of money involved, and there would be litigation. To keep Dow's name fairly clean, it was necessary to spend quite a lot of time sometimes, just to determine what the problem was. If it was volatility and they used the wrong 2,4-D product, that's different than if it's a spray drift. So the two things, volatility and spray drift, became real important. This is where a lot of work was done in our building up here in Midland, to develop equipment that would reduce spray drift".

Davidson remembered an incident during the early Dow experiments with 2,4-D. "It doesn't take much of an amount of it, in its volatile form, to damage a good crop, or good plants, any place", he said. "We found that out the hard way down in South Haven We'd been doing some work with some esters that were quite volatile, and the fellows had it all over their clothes. We were doing a test in the greenhouse, where they were also growing poinsettias. If you have worked around poinsettias you know that they are very sensitive to 2,4-D. These fellows came in -- this was 1947 or 1948 -- before we even realized the volatility of it very much, walking through this greenhouse with all of these poinsettias after they had been outside treating some stumps or something, and with just the stuff on their overalls, walking through this greenhouse, all those poinsettias dropped their leaves. We learned the hard way about the importance of volatility. It cost us some money -- we had to pay for the poinsettias. It was part of the business in those days".6

So far as 2,4,5-T was concerned, Davidson said, "several of us there at South Haven had worked with that ever since it became available, and you'd work with it in a rather careless manner much of the time. It never seemed to affect any of us very seriously, at least as far as we knew at the time. So I think it and the dioxin issue have been somewhat overblown, but there were certain formulations of 2,4,5-T -- formulations by certain manufacturers -- that did contain quite a bit more dioxin than Dow's, because we knew that dioxin was getting in there and we made quite a little effort to keep it down".

Most of Davidson's published papers (published in the technical literature) concerned nematodes. "One of the areas where nematodes were a real problem were certain nurseries where cherry trees were grown, where they'd been grown year after year, and in cherry orchards. Where they'd replanted cherry orchards, they were having trouble with the young trees growing, and by going in there and fumigating with ethylene dibromide we'd control the nematodes and the trees would grow much better, so we used to publish articles on that", he said.

151

His career even took him into helping the wild deer population. "One area we worked in quite extensively for a while was controlling unwanted vegetation in wildlife areas", he said. "I worked with the Michigan Department of Conservation in opening up areas in densely forested areas so that deer and other wildlife would flourish better in those open areas -- they don't like it where the forest is too dense".

He continued working full time until he was 72 years old. "They didn't ask me to quit, and I felt good and I wanted to keep working, so I said, okay", he said. "In fact, they didn't ask me to retire even then. I did it voluntarily".

By then he was thoroughly familiar with courtroom life and the role of technical adviser to the legal staff. "I'm sure that had something to do with my staying on", he said.

Charlie Fischer, a later leader of the Dow AgroScience business (about whom we will have more to say presently), said it was the contributions of people such as Davidson that made for the success of the enterprise. "There are a lot of great people that made it happen", he said. "Guys like John Davidson. John Davidson never sparkled as anybody's up-and-coming leader, but the guy would just continue to work for the benefit of the company through tough times and good times, and created a lot of value and probably never stood up and took any awards for anything. He was just a solid guy, and there's a whole bunch of them like that".[7]

Today, at age 92 and a widower, Davidson still follows the technical literature published by the American Chemical Society, the American Society of Horticultural Science, the Weed Science Society, and other scientific groups. "You have to keep up", he said.

PART THREE

THE MODERN ERA

1970 - 2007

PART THREE --
THE MODERN ERA
1970-2007

1970 -- Tordon for rangeland plant control is launched in the U.S. with registration in Texas, and use of this herbicide for controlling brush on utility rights-of-way is also growing rapidly.

1972 -- Polyethylene D is introduced by Dow. It is an insecticide-impregnated plastic film used to bag growing bananas, providing bigger, better bananas at less cost. Greatly improved bananas reach new heights of popularity as a staple of the American diet.

1973 -- Dursban becomes a major product and production capacity is tripled for this broad-range, ecologically sound insecticide. Plictran miticide is approved in the U.S. for preventing mite damage to apples, pears, and citrus.

1974 -- EPA moves to ban the use of 2,4,5-T, the key ingredient of Agent Orange, under fire for its use in the war in Vietnam. Dow prepares extensive data to show that 2,4,5-T's benefits greatly exceed any risks caused by its use. EPA withdraws its order and cancels a hearing it had called, deciding to conduct further research.

1975 -- A new Lontrel herbicide developed by Dow is the subject of field trials in 15 European countries. It is designed for weed control in small grain crops.

1976 -- Lorsban, a new insecticide designed for use by cotton and corn growers, is winning acceptance as an effective insect control agent.

1976 -- Start-up of a plant to produce N-Serve occurs at Pittsburg, California.

1977 -- Telone, a new soil fumigant, is among Dow's promising new products.

1979 -- Dow honors its top research scientists by awarding them the newly-minted Herbert H. Dow Medal for their achievements, including Howard Johnston, expert in chloropyridine chemistry, who developed a family of agricultural chemicals including N-Serve nitrogen stabilizer, and Tordon, Lontrel, and Garlon herbicides; and Raymond H. Rigterink, expert in the synthesis of heterocyclic molecules, whose work paved the way to such products as Coyden coccidiostat and Dursban, Lorsban, and Reldan insecticides.

1980 -- Garlon herbicide, used principally for utility lines and forestry control, goes into production. Dursban is being investigated, and shows promise, for termite control

1980 -- Dow acquires Prochim, a French formulator and marketer of agricultural chemicals since 1946, and forms a new French agricultural chemical firm called Prochimagro.

1982 -- Dow prepares to launch several new products although the U.S. farm economy is in a depression. They are Tandem herbicide, Garlon herbicide, and Dowco 453, a promising grass herbicide.

1983 -- Lorsban insecticide and Lontrel herbicide are introduced and gain broad acceptance in the marketplace.

1984 -- Dow launches Tandem, Verdict, and Starane.

1986 --- EPA grants registration of Tandem herbicide for control of weeds in corn, and it is introduced during the 1986 growing season. Starane herbicide, for small grains, is successfully launched in the U.K. and France, and joins Lontrel in Dow's product line for cereal grains.

1989 -- In April, Dow and Eli Lilly & Co., Indianapolis, announce the formation of DowElanco, world's sixth largest research-based agricultural chemical company, which includes the plant science businesses of both parents and Dow's industrial pest control business. Dow holds a 60% position in the new company. DowElanco projects $1.5 billion in sales in its first year. Its product line includes Balan, Flexidor, Garlon, Lontrel, Paarlan, Sonalan, Tordon, Treflan, Turflon, Verdict and Gallant herbicides; Beam, Rubigan and Trimidal fungicides; Cutless plant growth regulator, N-Serve nitrogen stabilizer, Telone soil fumigant, Vikane gas fumigant, and hybrid seeds; and Dursban, Lorsban, Nurelle and Reldan insecticides.

1990 -- Patent for active compounds used in Broadstrike and Pronto herbicides is issued to William Kleschik, Robert Ehr, Mark Costates, Ben Gerwick, Richard Meikle, William Monte, and Norman Pearson.

1991 -- DowElanco begins construction of a world-scale production plant in France. The company is particularly strong in Europe, with Starane, Lontrel, Lorsban, and Dursban as sales leaders.

1995 -- DowElanco awaits registration of Tracer naturalyte insect control.

1996 -- DowElanco aquires a majority interest in Mycogen Corp., and its United Agriseeds subsidiary becomes part of Mycogen, marking the firm's entry into agricultural biotechnology. DowElanco and Mycogen control the largest and deepest patent position for insect resistance in major crops.

1997 -- Dow purchases the 40% share of DowElanco owned by Eli Lilly & Co. for $900 million, and with Dow owning 100% of the firm it is renamed Dow AgroSciences LLC.

1997 -- Dow acquires full ownership of Sentrachem Ltd., based in South Africa, maker of specialty and agricultural chemicals.

1997 -- Tracer and Success insect control products achieve high customer acceptance.

1998 -- Dow forms an alliance with Illinois Foundation Seeds, which clears the way for the formation of AgriTrails LLC.

1999 -- In August, Dow and Union Carbide Corp. announce their merger, which is approved by UCC stockholders on December 1.

1999 -- Dow AgroSciences launches a series of new products, including Sentricon Termite Colony Elimination System, Tracer insecticide, FirstRate and Strongarm herbicides, and Fortress fungicide. It also launches a global glyphosate strategy that includes a manufacturing agreement with Monsanto Co. and formation of a manufacturing joint venture with Finagro S.p.A., an Italian firm.

2000 -- EPA honors Dow AgroSciences with its Green Chemistry Challenge Award for Spinosad, a revolutionary new insect control product derived from a naturally-occurring soil organism.

2000 -- Dow and Cargill Inc. form first world-scale polylactide facility to make plastics from agricultural crops.

2000 -- Dow AgroSciences and Cheminova A/S, a Danish manufacturer of farm chemicals, form a joint venture for the manufacture of pyrethroid insecticide.

2000 -- Dow AgroSciences acquires Acetochlor herbicide from Zeneca Ltd.

2001 -- Dow AgroSciences completes the acquisition of Rohm & Haas Co.'s agricultural business, and also acquires remaining interest in RohMid from BASF.

2002 -- EPA awards "Stratospheric Ozone Protection Award" to Dow AgroSciences LLC for the development of alternatives to methyl bromide, widely used fumigant..

2002 -- Dow AgroSciences receives approval from Japanese regulatory agencies for Herculex insect protection, a genetically-engineered trait that provides resistance to European corn borer, black cutworm and other insects in corn.

2003 -- Midland is chosen as site for manufacture of penoxsulam, a new sulfonamides-based rice herbicide which has received "Reduced Risk Pesticide Status" from the EPA.

2004 -- Mycogen Corp., biotechnology affiliate of Dow AgroSciences, is granted U.S. patent rights to glyphosate resistance in cotton, greatly strengthening its position in that field.

2005 -- Herculex receives full food and feed approval in the U.S.

2005 -- Aminopyralid, an advanced herbicide for specialty crops, receives registration from EPA in U.S. and from the Canadian Pest Management Regulatory Agency.

2006 -- Dow introduces Glutex brand products, designed to help stop the spread of deadly animal viruses such as Avian Influenza H5N1.

Howard Johnston

Chapter 13

Howard Johnston, Synthesis Chemist

Howard Johnston, who helped Cleve Goring and many others so greatly in their endeavors to beat the bugs and improve the yield of food crops, was one of the most brilliant chemists the Dow Chemical Company ever hired, and also one of the most modest.

"I had heard of his amazing success in finding and developing new and useful chemical compounds, and I was quite eager to meet this California scientific genius", said Jack C. Little, one of his colleagues. "When I asked him about his research, he simply referred me to the others around him and seemed more interested in talking about my research than his. After I got back home in Michigan and discussed it with my peers I reaffirmed that, yes, this was indeed the man who had done all these amazing things. I concluded then that Howard Johnston was one very modest individual".1

Johnston was born in Billings, Montana, one of the many places his father, a mining man who searched far and wide in the western U.S. for gold and other metals, took his family before moving on. Howard attended nine different high schools before he graduated but in spite of that became the first person in his family to attend college. As a teen ager he developed a passionate interest in science fiction, and he decided to become a scientist and help transform science fiction into scientific fact. He majored in chemistry at the University of California, Berkeley, and then joined the Dow company's Western Division at Pittsburg, California, where he was to spend his entire career. He took a leave from Dow to earn a master's degree in organic chemistry at Stanford University, and then returned to Dow in 1950.2

At Dow he invented dozens of products and earned 65 patents in the U.S. and nearly 200 abroad. Among them were bactericides, fungicides, insecticides, and herbicides. These products helped the world's farmers grow stronger, better plants, and some of his inventions battled pests, while others were fertilizers or helped plants to absorb nutrients better. "He was very gentle, and always helpful", said Walter Reifschneider, one of his fellow chemists and researchers. "He was a mentor for all of his co-workers". Reifschneider estimated that Johnston's inventions resulted in enough food to feed 100 million people all their lives.

In 1960, at a company research conference held at Seal Beach, California, Johnston introduced his colleagues to a precursor for what ultimately became Dursban insecticide, one of the most widely used, safest, broad-spectrum insecticides in the world, and raised the curtain on what became the company's most succesful modern agricultural chemical family, the chloropyridines.

When the Dow company introduced the gold Herbert H. Dow Medal in 1979 it presented the medal to six of its top chemical inventors, and Howard Johnston was one of them. Johnston's citation said the medal was conferred on him "...for his research contributions in the field of halogenated heterocyclic chemistry, and particularly for his work in chloropyridine chemistry".

It was deeply ironic, Jack Little said, that "although Howard was by nature a pacifist who hated war", some of his discoveries were used prominently in the Vietnam war. "The powerful herbicide picloram or Tordon, for example, was used by the military as Agent White to defoliate the jungles of Vietnam", he said. "Another Johnston product, Garlon, was a structural analog of the controversial 2,4,5-T or Agent Orange, ultimately replacing the latter as a commercial product because of its nearly identical spectrum and much greater biological activity".

His boyhood interest in science fiction stayed with him all his life. He believed in "fringe" science such as extra-sensory perception, parapsychology, and psychic studies. "Although he was a successful man of science", his son Brian said, "he had a fascination with the edge of what was known to science, and scorned those who felt science set limits on human potential or the wonder of the universe". 3

Brian said his father delighted his three children with a series of fanciful inventions that he made up from time to time especially for them. Brian's favorite was a miniature water tower that pumped water through a series of tiny tubes.

His work took him on trips to many parts of the world, and wherever Johnston went he came back with a pocketful of seeds. Over the years he and his wife, Virginia, planted more than 2,000 varieties of plants derived chiefly in this way on their hilly property in Walnut Creek, California, where he lived most of his adult life. "Not all of them survived", Virginia said. Eventually it grew into a lush, three-and-a-half acre garden with greenhouses called the Heather Farm Garden Center, where they raised and propagated all kinds of tropical species and cacti. It was a reflection of the many places they had gone and the many things they had seen, and it was there, in this place that he loved, that a funeral service for Johnston was held when he died at the age of 78 in 1999.

It was the search for a nitrogen stabilizer initiated by Cleve Goring that accidentally triggered the Dow researchers on the route to pyridine chemistry, as Johnston and others have noted. The pyridines originated in great mixtures, which most chemists wanted nothing to do with, and, as Johnston said, "the trouble was that (this mixture) contained a lot of other things which were very difficult to separate from the mixture. (Later research showed that the mixture contained at least 12 different pyridine compounds). It was these other things which gave us insurmountable problems for use as a nitirogen stabilizer but at the same time led to the discovery of many of the products based on pyridine that we have today".4

This resulted in a joint research program involving John Kagy's group at Seal Beach (later at Walnut Creek), and the chemists at Pittsburg. "This cooperation extended over many years, in the course of which a number of important products and processes were discovered or developed", he said. "Some of these were N-Serve, Tordon, Lontrel, Garlon, the preservatives S-13 and A-40, pentachloro pyridine, Sym-Tet, and the Dursban precursor 3,5,6-trichloro-2-pyridinol"

"He seemed to have a thorough understanding of how plants and organisms interacted and how his own discoveries might affect them", Little said. "I frequently accused him of having chats with Mother Nature herself, because he always arrived at work early in the morning, often the first person on the site".

The pyridine family that Johnston developed, which resulted in sales of over $1 billion by Dow annually, includes the first product to be commercialized, Tordon herbicide (or picloram), Lorsban and Dursban insecticide (chlorpyrifos), at one time the world's largest-selling organophosphate insecticide, Stinger herbicide (clopyralid), Starane herbicide (fluroxypyr), Verdict herbicide (haloxyfop), and Garlon herbicide (triclopyr).

"This chemistry was developed by a dedicated, forward-looking team that was eager to bring the next generation of agricultural chemistry to the marketplace", said Richard M (Rick). Gross, then vice president and director of research and development for Dow, in 1999.5

In the twilight of his career Johnston was showered with honors. He was promoted to Dow Fellow, the highest position available to a Dow scientist and, as has been mentioned, awarded the Herbert H. Dow Medal, the highest scientific award given by the Dow company for outstanding achievement. In 1986 he was inducted into the California Inventors Hall of Fame, and in 1999 was acclaimed a "Hero of Chemistry" by the American Chemical Society

"Because of his almost self-effacing modesty, relatively few people who knew Howard outside his research environment were aware of these accomplishments", Little said. "He persisted, almost to a fault, in giving credit for his discoveries to his co-workers and associates, studiously avoiding the limelight whenever possible".

The chemistry created by Johnston and his fellow chemists "affects nearly every phase of food production and industrial control around the globe", said Len Smith, former Dow AgroSciences vice president. "They dramatically improved the health and welfare of millions of people worldwide, from crop protection in corn and soybean fields in Indiana to insect control in densely populated cities like Tokyo".6

Julius E. Johnson

Chapter 14

Julius Johnson, the mountain climber

In 1936, when he was 19, Julius Johnson and a fellow student at Colorado University, Carl Melzer, followed the crest of the Continental Divide on foot from the state of Wyoming to the state of New Mexico, a distance of about 750 miles. It took them two months and got them a lot of publicity. The next year he and Melzer climbed 37 mountains of 14,000 feet or more, and then he hurt his foot and had to quit for a time. Colorado University offered a program of hikes and climbs for summer students, and he was head guide for the program for four years.

His mountain-climbing skills came to be highly useful when he joined the Dow Chemical Company in 1943, although the mountains he was called upon to climb were of a different sort than the Rockies.

"Those years as a mountain guide, especially guiding large groups of people, were memorable", Johnson said. "We'd take up to 30 people on a climb of Longs Peak. Each weekend was a different climb, rain or shine, wet camps and dry. The most I ever guided was 300 people up to the Arapaho Glacier, a one-day trip. We'd climb the trail to the saddle by South Arapaho, encourage everyone to slide down the glacier on the seat of their pants, and then dry out on the way home. We had a great time. I learned a lot, about speaking to groups and motivating recalcitrant people. It was a very important part of my experience".1

He was inspired to go into chemistry by Reuben G. (Gus) Gustavson, head of the chemistry department at Colorado, "one of the most inspiring teachers who ever existed", he called him. During his senior year at Colorado Gus called him into his office and told Johnson, "I have a letter from William C. Rose at (the University of) Illinois looking for a graduate student on a fellowship funded by the Rockefeller Foundation. (Rose was famous as the biochemist who first isolated and characterized threonine, an essential amino acid in protein). I've done all I can for you, and if you go to Illinois you'll be with the very cream of the crop as far as chemistry is concerned. Rose is a top man, and Roger Adams, Reynold C. Fuson, and Carl S. (Speed) Marvel are all among the very best in the country. I recommend you do it".

"I didn't think very long about making an application", Johnson said. "It was $500 a year -- 10 months at $50 a month -- plus tuition and fees. I paid for my books, room and board, and transportation, and saved money!"

He earned his Ph.D. with Dr. Rose in 1943.

He interviewed with four companies for a job, and rather quickly chose to accept a position with Dow Chemical after interviewing with Dr. Don D. Irish, who had established Dow's Toxicology Laboratory in 1933. "Dow had a consultative arrangement and antimalarial program underway with Dr. A. P. Richardson of the University of Tennessee Medical School at Memphis, a project organized in cooperation with a national program searching for antimalarial drugs. America's quinine supplies had been cut off by the Japanese during their early successes after the Pearl Harbor attack.

"Don Irish wanted to establish testing procedures whereby Dow could examine some 3,000 new compounds that Dow then had to see if they had anti-malarial activity", Johnson said. "When I heard about this possible job it seemed not exactly down the line of my biochemical training; but a project that was very worthwhile. I was impressed with Irish, with his enthusiasm, and with the other Dow men I met. I didn't consider the other jobs I had interviewed for any further. That's how I got started at Dow. The antimalarial project did qualify me for deferment from the draft. I explained to the draft board what I was doing, and I felt I was making good use of my trade".

The search for anti-malaria compounds petered out as the war wound down, especially with the spectacular successes the U.S. military was having with DDT, eliminating in many parts of the world the mosquitoes who carried the malady. "We found several compounds which were active (against malaria)", Johnson said, "but none active enough or safe enough to be used in man. We did see some possibilities of products for the control of parasites in man".

After the war, the companies who had conducted research on antimalarials "were gearing up to test their compounds as coccidiostats, which could be sold to the poultry industry", he said. Coccidiosis is the most common disease and one of the biggest problems of the poultry industry. Dow and Johnson joined the hunt for a coccidiostat.

"The coccidial organism is quite similar to malaria in its life history", Johnson said.
"Coccidia affect animals and birds. The primary economic impact was with chickens. As soon as chickens are crowded together in boiler houses this parasitic disease causes high mortality and lowered production efficiency".

There was growing interest in the poultry industry in Dow at that time because Dr. E. C. Britton had developed ways of manufacturing all of the essential amino acids in his laboratory, including methionine. "This amino acid is deficient in all poultry feeds", Johnson said. "The lowest cost feed, made with combinations of corn and soybean meal, doesn't contain enough methionine. The way to supply methionine was to add fish meal or other expensive, methionine-rich ingredients. Synthetic methionine was a lower-cost answer".

Additionally, Dow had a small entree to the coccidiostat market because Dr. Britton had made phenylsulfonic acids for Salisbury Laboratories, which manufactured drinking water tablets used with poultry to control parasites.

So Julius Johnson, with the help of an assistant, Dorsey Mussell, set out on a search for a coccidiostat. "We tested many compounds for coccidiosis control", he said, using a test devised by their colleague Dr. Theo Hymas which was then added to routine new compound evaluations in the agricultural field for insecticidal, fungicidal, miticidal, and herbicidal activity.

Among the Dow researchers it was a California group headed by W. E. (Bill) Brown, Guy Harris, and Bryant Fischback who came up with Dow's first coccidiostat, which they called Zoalene.2 It was sold as a 25 per cent concentrate mixed into poultry feed which was then called Zoamix. Johnson went to New York to present a paper on the new product at the New York Academy of Sciences. "It turned out that the meeting was orchestrated by Dr. Sterling Brackett of the American Cyanamid

Corporation", he said. "I learned, to my regret, that Cyanamid had a superior coccidiostat to announce at that meeting. Our product didn't even come close to the efficacy of theirs. Merck also had a good product to announce at that time. So we at Dow went back to the drawing boards and in a few years came out with two superior products. Those were developed for the market by Theo Hymas and Hollis Brower".

As it turned out, resistance to coccidiostats began to show up in flocks when they were fed the same medication for some time, and for this reason poultry disease specialists urged poultrymen to alternate the medications given to their flocks. Zoalene turned out to be a winner, after all.3

In 1952 Dow president Leland I. Doan decided (at the suggestion of his son and successor, H. D. (Ted) Doan) that it was time to set up agricultural chemicals as a separate and distinct division of the company, and he assigned J. W. (Bill) Britton (half-brother of Dr. Edgar C. Britton) to take over and organize the new division. The J. W. stood for Joseph Walter, but he had been known as "Bill" since his boyhood days in Rockville, Indiana. He was a veteran production manager at the Dow plant in Midland, having been with the company since 1923, almost entirely in a production role.

"Life is a series of improbabilities", Bill Britton often said.

As one of his first acts, Britton promoted Johnson to be the new department's director of research and development. It was the first time the "aggies" had had one; up to this time the responsibility for researching new agricultural chemical products had been shared between Don Irish and E. C. Britton. "Bill Britton was a marvelous man", Johnson said. "I've never enjoyed working for a man quite as much as I did for him".

Another of Britton's first moves was to establish a Technical Service and Development group, responding to the need for technical agricultural personnel in the field to back up the sales contingent and to maintain contact with public agency personnel. Larry Southwick was the first assigned this responsibility, based in Midland. Hoyt Nation was hired to serve the Southeastern U.S. The marketing function had already been reorganized beginning in 1948, when William W. Allen had been assigned duties as manager of Agricultural Chemical Sales. It was a job he would hold for 16 years.

Johnson asked Keith Barrons to manage the field research and development function. Fred Fletcher was assigned responsibility for insecticide and miticide development. Chet Otis was moved to Midland to take charge of herbicide development, and Dick Raynor was added as an herbicide specialist. Theo Hymas took over the management of coccidiostat development. Hollis Brower, who had poultry-feed experience with Ralston-Purina, was assigned to work with Hymas. The plant science research group under George E. (Lefty) Lynn, in Irish's laboratory, moved to the new division, as did the field work being done at South Haven, Michigan, under Walter Dutton, the western U. S. research being done at the Seal Beach, California, laboratory under John F. Kagy, and the laboratory and field station for animal research at Freeport, Texas.

Agricultural Chemicals was now for the first time on an equal footing with chemicals, plastics, and metals, the other major product groups of the company.

Johnson recounted what it was like working with Bill Britton. "We went to Europe in 1955 to survey prospects for Ag Chemical ventures. One of our contacts was Walter Ripper, a Brit since killed in a plane accident. Ripper was trying to make an impression on us because he wanted a relationship with Dow. He took Wendell Mullison (Dow's chief plant physiologist), Britton and me to his country estate near King's Lynn (in Eastern England). After dinner and brandies and endless bottles of Seltzer water, which Ripper claimed was supposed to clear your brain, we went to bed. Bill Britton, being highest in rank, got the Blue Room and Wendell and I got lesser rooms. Next morning I woke up and discovered that a maid had come in and lit a fire in the fireplace in my room. I was getting out of bed when a knock came at the door. In came Bill Britton. He looked at the fire and said, 'Damn this protocol anyway. They give me the Blue Room but they give you the fireplace'. Bill shivered all over England. It was May. We'd walk into a contact's office and he'd have the windows wide open, and there our host would be sitting with red cheeks and a sweater. The trip began to wear Britton down. One morning, in the lobby of the Westbury Hotel in London, I laid my key on the counter for the concierge and said, 'Bill, don't you want to leave your key?' He said, 'Hell no!! I want them to know where to ship the body!' Bill could tell many stories the likes of which you wouldn't believe. But when a lady came into the room, his behavior was punctilious, gracious, and as gentlemanly as you ever saw. Bill was a delight to be around".

The new agricultural chemicals department of Dow underwent its baptism by fire soon after it was established. "Keith Barrons at South Haven had discovered that DNOSBP 4 was a good pre-emergent herbicide", Johnson said. "This was a new concept, spraying after planting but before the weeds sprout and emerge. This compound, called Premerge, had been tested for about five years in the field. In 1952 Dow initiated a sales program for weed control in cotton using Premerge. This was promoted by the then head of Technical Service and Development C. B. (Ben) Branch. (Branch later became president and CEO of Dow, 1970-1976). The weather conditions were hot and dry. Our sales people began to receive reports of cotton plants dying soon after emergence, when they were an inch-and-a-half or two inches high. I had only recently accepted the job with Bill Britton. I told Bill, 'I haven't been involved yet, but I want to get down there and learn what's going on'. So I went down to Greenville, Mississippi, which was the base of operations for the (Dow) investigation team. Keith Barrons, Larry Southwick, Hoyt Nation, and others, and a group from the West coast were there,. We had about 20 Dow people there, who fanned out over the Mississippi delta -- Mississippi and Arkansas, primarily -- and followed up on each of the complaints to see if we couldn't find out what was wrong. We finally concluded that during the five years of testing we had never had severe hot weather conditions, and that the hot weather was causing the herbicide to volatilize off the hot soil and kill the very young cotton shoots. Although it was a very rare occurrence, these adverse conditions did happen in 1952 on a massive scale. When the Dow people had analyzed the problem and found the probable cause, the company offered to replace the product on replanting."

It fell upon Ben Branch to persuade the Dow Executive Committee, back in Midland, to do this. "The seedling cotton was limp in the fields, acre after acre of it", Branch said. "I got back to Midland and the next morning I saw Lee Doan and told him the story. I went to the Executive Committee meeting and told them my story. Someone asked, 'What will it cost us?' I said if the growers had applied all the Premerge we had sold in the area, and if the damage could be blamed on the chemical rather than a plant disease, the cost conceivably could run as high as $20 million".5

As it turned out, Branch said, "the damage cost the company only $250,000, but no one ever blamed me....We learned a lot from that incident, and made sure it would never be repeated. But from that time on, I also knew I had nothing to fear from making a mistake that the company could live with".

Johnson said the experience taught him two things. "First of all, pay attention to Murphy's Law. And second, if you've got a problem, then pour in the resources quickly, get facts quickly, and show sustained interest before people start spreading rumors and thinking that you're running for cover. It worked in 1952. That was my introduction to practical problems in agricultural chemicals".

His 10 years as director of agricultural chemical research "were the best in my life", Johnson said. "I thoroughly enjoyed them".

Early in his tenure he perceived that with many research projects going on, at different stages of development, that the progress of research needed to be better defined. With the help of Kagy, Dutton, and Francis N. (Al) Alquist, a chemist in the Britton Lab, "we created a staging system to define the progress of our research projects", he said. "Before that we were always talking about, 'Well, this is a laboratory test, this is a first-stage field test, this is a more elaborate test, this is a confirmatory test with a grower'. We were using lots of words. So we decided to define these steps. 'Stage 1' was exploration for potentially useful compounds. 'Stage 2' was quantification under laboratory conditions to establish dosages and breakpoints and early indications of toxicity. 'Stage 3' focused on serious and expensive field tests that require a lot of planning and effort and preparation for collecting of residue samples. 'Stage 4' was work with cooperators in the experiment stations with attendant work on the analysis and toxicology; and 'Stage 5' was initial sales. Promotion from stage to stage required a review of checklists to make sure that we weren't forgetting an important test or procedure or approval"

This system was instituted immediately in the ag chem department, he said. "With our decentralized organization this was very helpful, even

173

though it was bureaucratic". Later on, when Johnson became Dow vice president for research and development, it was applied to the entire company, but not as formally. "When I was giving reports to the Board of Directors I would define the stages to the board", he said. "They knew that when I talked of a Stage 1, that the odds of success might be one in a hundred; in Stage 2, somewhat better. So that became standard terminology, to a certain extent".

Another thing that was appended to that, or was an alternative to it, he said with a smile, was what was called a SWAG, which meant Scientific Wild Ass Guess. These were scientifically-based guesses about the potential of a research project made by the business teams and the project management teams. "When we were trying to put an economic interpretation on where a research project stood, so that, come budget time, we could judge priorities, a SWAG was sometimes used. Those projects at the bottom of the SWAG list were most likely to be cut".

"But, as you can imagine, formalization rubbed a lot of research people the wrong way", Johnson said. "'This is stereotyping, this is putting us in straitjackets', they would say. But there was a discipline to it. Some of the opponents who hated SWAG tried to terminate both SWAG and the stage system, but as far as I know the system has survived".

The basic objective of the system "was part of the budgeting process to try to appraise whether we were putting our money in the best opportunities short and long term", he said.

"We set aside about 15 per cent of the research budget for exploratory research not subject to this kind of hassle", Johnson said. "But when a product emerged in Stage 1, we began to apply some marketing thinking and manufacturing thinking to it. Is this going to be a feasible thing to make or is it going to cause some big problems? And during this whole process we tried to think of questions like, 'Do we have the raw materials? Do we have a process to make it? Do we have a position of uniqueness (at best, a patent)? Do we have a position in marketing? If it's a system, do we have the components of the system? Any one of these factors could be so dominant that it might carry the decision, but all of them should be considered."

When Bill Britton retired in 1962 at age 66, Johnson succeeded him as chief of the agricultural chemical department of Dow. He had climbed another mountain. Johnson combined the research and development functions of the department but separated plant science products from animal health products. Keith Barrons was made director of plant science R & D and Theo Hymas was made director of animal science R & D. Lefty Lynn supervised the registration activities for both groups. "Barrons and Hymas each capably handled their roles, without much attention from me", Johnson said.

In the early 1960's Ted Doan was expanding the company's activities in the pharmaceutical area, first with the acquisition of the Pitman-Moore Company in 1960 (Pitman-Moore was a leading name in the veterinary medicine field), and then with the Italian Lepetit firm in 1964. Doan lumped the pharmaceutical products with agricultural chemicals and it became the Bioproducts department of Dow, with Julius Johnson as manager.

It was also during this period that agricultural chemicals came into the limelight as part of the public's rapidly rising awareness of problems associated with the environment, which awareness had been triggered by the publication of Rachel Carson's book, "Silent Spring", in 1962. "My first involvement with the U.S. government in a major way was in 1963, when I was manager of agricultural chemicals", Johnson said. "As a result (of the Carson book), the National Agricultural Chemicals Association, an association of companies selling agricultural chemicals, had been asked by Sen. Abraham Ribicoff (of Connecticut) to defend practices in the agricultural chemicals business before his committee, the Committee on Government Operations. He was trying to clarify the kind of safety studies different companies used during the development of their products. I went to the first hearing as a support person, there to answer questions if asked. My cohorts and I weren't asked, but the executive director of the NACA did a miserable job. Our industry emerged looking like a bunch of dummies. Fred Hatch, who was with Monsanto at the time, prevailed on the Ribicoff Committee to give us another chance but this time to have four separate companies independently report on what they individually were doing. This would give a much clearer picture. Practices vary a lot and each company must speak for itself.6

"I worked hard on testimony showing that Dow had developed methods for discovering, staging, studying the toxicology, analyzing, etc., the safety of our products. For a visual aid I used a long window shade four feet wide and sixty feet long, divided into sections about two feet wide, each representing a calendar quarter in time. I listed all the events that were taking place in the development of a new pesticide from discovery to launch. (This was a time when the launching of rockets was in vogue). We'd show what was done in Stage 1 by calendar quarters, in Stage 2 by calendar quarters, and everytime a praocedure involved safety, this was printed in green so it would stand out. Our first tests on safety began in Stage 2, when we'd run preliminary toxicology tests. We'd test algae, daphnia, or fish for aquatic toxicity; we'd also test sensitive plants. In Stage 3 there were more refined experiments, experiments for carcinogens, mutagens, teratogens, etc., all the way through to launch. The chart represented about seven years in time.

"You've seen Senate hearings, no doubt, when the witness is badgered by the committee. I was badgered especially by the assistant to Sen. Ribicoff, a fellow by the name of Jerry Sonofsky. He sat behind Ribicoff. He'd write a note on a 3x5 card and hand it over to the Senator and get a big smile on his face as though to say, 'Gotcha!' I'd answer the question, Sonofsky's face would fall, and he'd fill out another card. We did this for about 20 minutes. Finally I said, 'Senator, a lot of these questions are going to be answered if I can proceed with this chart'. By that time I had about 20 feet of the chart unrolled. Ribicoff let me go on. The full 60 feet went right down one side of the hearing room and halfway across the end, held up from behind by my colleagues. I concluded by saying that 'if you look at the green you can see that we are paying attention to safety from the very early stages (of the development of a product) through to its development and sale'."

That was Julius Johnson's initiation into the fine art of jousting with the U.S. government. "In May, 1969", he remembered, "I was invited by Emil Mrak, chancellor of the University of California at Davis, to join a committee being appointed by the secretary of the department of Health, Education, and Welfare, to investigate pesticides and their effect on man and the environment. Mrak was the most effective chairman I've ever seen. He completed what still is a landmark report by early November, 1969. I was in the section which looked at effects of pesticides on nontarget organisms. I learned a lot from the other people on the committee and was pleased to discover that Dow, compared to others, had not been insensitive to environmental matters. One of the key figures working with Dow pesticides had been Eugene Kenaga, who worked in the Agricultural lab in the early years with Lynn, Fletcher, and Irish. He was an entomologist by profession but an ornithologist by hobby, and a good one. As a result, Kenaga had developed an intense interest in the harmful effects of pesticides. He and Tom Powers of Dow (its first manager of pollution control) separately had done early experimental testing of chemicals on fish, algae, and daphnia. Kenaga was well-known to members of the Mrak Commission.

"Just before the final meeting of that commission, the news broke about Agent Orange causing birth defects in rats and being blamed for birth defects in Viet Nam. I returned to Midland and talked to V. K. Rowe and George Lynn and asked, 'What do you think is going on here?' V. K. said, 'I wonder if the 2,4,5-T they're using in Agent Orange is contaminated with 2,3,7,8-tetrachlorodibenzoparadioxin.' (This is now called dioxin for short). Rowe brought me up to date on some of the things he knew but I did not. We tracked down the sample of 2,4,5-T that had been tested in the Bionetics Laboratory at the Research Triangle in North Carolina. It came from Diamond Alkali. Diane Courtney was the researcher who ran the test at Bionetics. We obtained a portion of the same sample she used for analysis and found 20 parts per million of dioxin in that sample. In 1940-41 Dow had learned to bioassay for dioxin. The method would detect one part per million and was used to monitor quality. By 1969 more sophisticated analytical methods were available. One part per million was considered to be a safe amount and exposure (to that much) would not be hazardous. Rowe and Lynn helped me to gather the needed toxicity data. Just before the final meeting of the Mrak Commission, I asked Mrak to convene a small group and I told them what was known. The Defense Department had been advised previously of the possibility of dioxin contamination but the level was not considered hazardous, especially at one part per million.

"That same night, after that meeting, two events happened simultaneously. First, a group broke into Dow's Washington, D.C., office and threw files out the window and poured blood into other files. Second, a group broke into Dow's Computation Laboratory tape storage room in Midland and ran a magnet over a number of tapes to destroy the records. These vandals didn't destroy anything of value to Dow but did destroy the records of the local blood banks. These events happened simultaneously, and I began to wonder if there was some conspiracy afloat, a momentary thought which evaporated. It seemed that everything was happening according to some perverse plan."

Around this time Johnson read in the Wall Street Journal that Sen. Gaylord Nelson was proclaiming the first Earth Day, to be celebrated March 24, 1970. When he read that, "the idea of an Ecology Council occurred to me", he said. "At a Dow board of directors meeting in November, 1969, I proposed, 'Why don't we establish a council of individuals primarily responsible for bringing together the resources of the company, thinking about pollution and ecology issues, and planning how we're going to cope with these concerns'. At the beginning of 1970 we selected Chet Otis as director of the Ecology Council. That proved to be one of the best things we could have done because it involved all these otherwise insulated key managers who hadn't had to cope with Washington on the emerging issues. It stimulated people wanting to really pitch in and do what they could on environmental cleanup. The Ecology Council quickly took root. We also established an Environmental Technical Advisory Board (ETAB), a small group of people who could analyze problems and develop some rational ideas about how to approach them. The Ecology Council proved to be one of the activities I'm proudest of. It helped to put Dow ahead of the pack".

When Ray Boundy retired in 1968, Julius Johnson succeeded him, becoming the Dow company's second vice president for research and development. (Boundy was the first). He was also named to the Dow board of directors at that time, and served as a member of that group until 1978. He also served on several commissions of the National Academy of Sciences, including its International Environmental Programs Committee and its Board on Toxicology and Environmental Health Hazards, as well as various committees of the Environmental Protection Agency of the U.S. government, including its Health Effects Research Study and the executive committee of its Science Advisory Board.

Fortunately, he had learned how to climb mountains a long time before.

"Douglas Costle, when he was head of EPA, even considered me as a candidate to serve as the Director of Researach for EPA", Johnson said. "This was tempting but we mutually agreed that the activist flak would be a big hindrance. Later, Costle's successor, William Ruckelshaus, appointed me chairman of the Science Advisory Board for EPA. Whenever the subject of Agent Orange arose I offered to absent myself but in every case the committee members preferred that I stay in the meeting".

Recently, in honor of his ninetieth birthday, his "aggie" friends and colleagues, some three dozen of them, gathered at the old agricultural chemical headquarters building in Midland and burned a DVD on which each one in turn recalled some incident of their careers as an "aggie", and sent it to Julius. In response he sent them an eight-page summary of his Dow experiences entitled , "Life is a Series of Improbabilities". "Working for Dow and with the likes of you has been a rewarding and satisfying life for me...and I thank you sincerely", he wrote. "Most important was the collection of talented people (I worked with) who reliably demonstrated a high level of personal integrity".7

John Hagaman

Chapter 15

John Hagaman and Consolidation

The development of the farm chemical business followed much the same pattern in many of the world's larger chemical and petroleum companies as it did at Dow Chemical, starting out with a product or two -- a by-product or a serendipitous discovery -- to serve the agricultural market and growing up over time into a multi-product department or division of the company devoted exclusively to agricultural chemicals. For a long time this was a fragmented and somewhat disjointed industry composed mainly of the ag chemical departments of the large chemical and petroleum and pharmaceutical firms, plus a host of small specialty chemical outfits.

In the 1970's and 1980's a consolidation of these fragments of the ag chemical business began to take place, worldwide. Pieces of the industry were slapped or welded together into ever larger entities, in the hope and expectation that this would enable them to achieve greater business efficiency, better economics and effectiveness, and a more powerful push to aid and abet the world's farmers.

Casual entry into the farm chemical market rapidly became a thing of the past. The field was becoming more and more intensely competitive. To field a valid firm now required a critical mass large enough to support the increasingly heavy expense of research for new and better products, the increasingly heavy burden of environmental tests required by the EPA and other branches of government to ensure that the product would not harm beasts or birds or plants or fish, the associated costs of registering and marketing and advertising, and the increasingly heavy expense of a legal staff and insurance protection against lawsuits, which were often brought about through misuse of the product or other reasons out of the control of the industry. You just had to get bigger to survive, the experts said.

Of all these factors, perhaps the most critical was the need for research. New products were being introduced more and more frequently and on occasion a newer and better product would hit the marketplace before a company had recouped its expenses for the research and other investments it had made in its most recent new product, sometimes over a number of years.

.

"Consolidation (in the industry) had been taking place for a number of years", said John Hagaman, a key figure in this development at Dow . "Du Pont bought Shell's U.S. ag business. Rhone-Poulenc bought Union Carbide's ag business. Chevron first formed a joint venture with Sumitomo, then sold their part of the joint venture to Sumitomo, so Chevron's ag business went to Sumitomo. It goes on and on. If you look at the list of ag chemical companies today, it looks a lot different than it did 10 years ago".1

"We had been talking about and had been investigating acquisitions, alliances, and joint ventures for some period of time", Hagaman said. "In fact, we had talked with Eli Lilly (a major pharmaceutical firm headquartered in Indianapolis, Indiana), about joining together the ag businesses (of Dow and Eli Lilly) back in late 1983 or early 1984. We had some very serious talks with Eli Lilly at that time, and while those talks did not end in a successful venture, they ended with both companies having a very high level of respect for the other. Both companies felt that 'here's a company we can get along with'. They ended very cordially and friendly even though we ended up agreeing not to agree.

"In February of 1989 I contacted my counterpart in Eli Lilly (Edward R. Roberts, president of Elanco Products Company, the agricultural division of Eli Lilly & Co.) and said, 'You know, the industry hasn't changed. The need for consolidation is still the same. Is there a basis for us to talk again?' That initiated talks. We made the first contact in early February. We had the first talks in late February, and we signed a preliminary agreement in April. We signed a definitive agreement in August and we closed the transaction in November, or the end of October. So it went very rapidly. One of the reasons it went rapidly is because we had had negotiations before and a lot of the groundwork had been laid"

The joint venture was announced April 18, 1989. "It was a significant event when Eli Lilly said, 'Yes, we can live with it. We can accept a situation where we are a minority interest'. That was a significant step in the discussions", Hagaman said. It was also incidentally the date it was announced that he would be the president and CEO of the new firm, which was called "DowElanco". With sales in its first year of $1.5 billion it became the sixth largest research-based agricultural company in the world. With Dow sales alone, it had been tenth.2

"We agreed that we would value the businesses, and then we would set the percentages (to be owned by each parent company) based on the value of the businesses", Hagaman said "It was known at that time that this would result in Dow having a majority share". When the legal underbrush had been cleared away it turned out that Dow would own 60 per cent of the firm, and Eli Lilly & Co., 40 per cent. Eli Lilly had the option of selling its share to Dow, if and when it wished to do so, an option it eventually exercised eight years later, in 1997, when it sold its share of DowElanco to Dow for $900 million..

The combination of the two organizations went "quite well", Hagaman said. "I think the people from both companies realized the need to have the consolidation. They understood the business and they understood why the venture was done. Because they understood the industry, and why the industry was consolidating, they understood that both of us (standing alone) were sub-scale. They knew that some form of acquisition, alliance, merger, or something was going to be necessary.

The new firm had a product line including 12 different kinds and brands of herbicides, four different insecticides, three kinds of fungicides, gas and soil fumigants, a plant growth regulator and a nitrogen stabilizer. The Elanco side brought with it what had been called "one of the most successful ag products of all time", Treflan, or trifluralin, a herbicide for cotton fields and soybeans.3

"Treflan had been a hugely profitable product for Lilly and, I imagine, provided very important cash flow to help fund their pharmaceutical research in the 1970's", said Charlie Fischer, John Hagaman's successor at the helm of Dow Agrosciences. "It was a revolutionary product, but Lilly had decided to move on from plant science research, and we (Dow) benefited. Now, having said that, we soon learned that Treflan's day had passed and the downside of this joint venture was that Treflan went down faster than we had expected in our analysis".

"I'd say that Lilly was probably as good a partner as we could ever have anticipated", Fisher said. "They were supportive of growth in DowElanco, even though they knew from the start that there was going to be a time of divestment. I think they entered into a joint venture instead of just selling it to us for two reasons. First, they didn't need the money when they did the deal, but could get an option to sell their property for cash whenever it fit their needs. Second, I think company. So in their agreement with us they said, 'We'll take the forty percent. We'll take two votes instead of three on the board (the five-person board of directors had three Dow representatives and two Eli Lilly), but on people issues in the first five years, it'll be a fifty-fifty vote. We will have as much say about the people and how they're handled as you will in the first five years' They did, and it paid off for the Lilly employees and in my opinion for the new enterprise. Many former Lilly people fill very important in our organization today. I think in the industry, this joint venture is seen as one of the most successful ag mergers. Lilly got what they wanted. They eventually sold it to Dow for a good price the year they needed to sell it. Their people got treated fairly. But during the time we were partners they never once withheld on an investment that we wanted to make – they would always help the management of Dow Elanco. When Dow became maybe too dominant on an issues, they would say, 'Hey, wait. We want to say something about this one.' It was just a great relationship and I think that Lilly people are very proud of what they did".

"In my perspective, John Hagaman has to be given credit as on o the greatest change agents in Dow ag because he was the guy that made the DowElanco joint venture happen, along with Clayton S. Williams and John C. Lilluch", Fischer said. "Those three guys made that happen and should be given credit for that. Without the DowElanco joint venture I have some doubt that Dow would be a viable player in the industry today".

The new firm moved into temporary quarters in Indianapolis in the summer of 1989 (the effective date of the merger was August 31, 1989) and immediately began planning and building a new corporate headquarters and research center in the same city. When it was completed in 1994 it was hailed as the largest agricultural and specialty research operation under one roof in the world.

Among the other gee-whiz facets of this new facility, the new research center had computer-operated greenhouses that could simulate the growing conditions almost anyplace in the world, ranging from, for example, a 40-degree day for winter wheat in South Dakota to a 90-degree day with high humidity for rice growing in the Far East. Field stations for testing out products in various climates were no longer really needed.

It was a startling contrast to the bleak and grimy little laboratory at Seal Beach, California, that John Kagy had set up as Dow's first exclusively ag chemical research center, 50 years before.

In the meantime the new firm also built a big new research laboratory for the European market, located in Drusenheim, France, and completed in 1992.

John Hagaman came to the leadership of Dow Agro, as it came to be known, by a roundabout route. He was born on his father's ranch, raising Hereford cattle and angora goats, at Ranger, Texas. He was the only son, and he was 18 and about to leave for college when his father unexpectedly died. He went off to Texas A & M university, where his father had gone, assuming he would be running the family ranch when he had finished. But by the time he was a senior his ideas had changed radically, and he signed up instead for interviews with several possible employers, among them Dow Chemical.

"They (Dow's interviewers) recommended me, and I came then to Midland, Michigan, for my third interview", he remembered. "It was early February and I thought I had gone to the North Pole. I had never been anywhere close to as far north as Michigan, and never in the wintertime. But I interviewed and was offered a job and took it".

The recruiter for another company, he remembered, had asked him who else he was interviewing. Hagaman told him he had interviewed three or four other companies "but I'm waiting for an answer from Ralston Purina and from Dow". The recruiter said, "Well, we'd love to have you come to work for us, but if you get an offer from Dow you ought to take it".

When he emerged from the sales training program at Dow he was assigned to the merchandising section of the ag department, directed by Clyde

Bryant, which was responsible for creating marketing and promotional programs. A year or two later he was switched to field sales in Houston, and became a field salesman for east Texas and Oklahoma, working primarily with cattle and grain ranchers. It involved a lot of travel, he said, and "lots of times I wouldn't even bring my car back home on a weekend. If I was in Oklahoma, I would tend to leave my car in Tulsa or Oklahoma City and fly back home on a Friday night, go into the office Monday morning and turn in the expense account, and then fly back to Tulsa or Oklahoma City and start again".

In 1967 he got a phone call from Clyde Bryant, who in the interim had gone out to Hong Kong to become the first ag manager of Dow for the Pacific area. Hong Kong was the hub of Dow's Far Eastern activities. Would John like to come out to the Far East, Bryant asked, and work on the development of Dow's ag business in that part of the world? He immediately said he would.

Both he and his wife, Nelda -- he had married his high school sweetheart -- saw Hong Kong as an opportunity, and they welcomed it. "I loved Hong Kong the minute I got off the airplane", he said. "I felt at home in Hong Kong the minute I got off the airplane and it has never changed"

Bryant asked him to take over the sales of Dow's ag products for the vast territory of "Asia". His title was assistant marketing manager for pharmaceuticals, agricultural, and consumer products (PAC) for the Pacific area. "At that time the Pacific area was broken up into three regions", Hagaman said. "There was Japan and Korea in the north, Australia and New Zealand in the south, and kind of everything else, Asia, in the middle...Where we had offices, I would work with the offices that we had. But we didn't have an office in Indonesia at that time. We didn't have one in Pakistan at that time. Where there weren't Dow people I would work with the distributors. Where there weren't distributors I would sign up a distributor....And the PRC (People's Republic of China) was not part of the equation then -- at that time, anyway. PRC was closed".

In hindsight, he said many years later, all these things seemed more like opportunities than problems at the time. "You just kind of had a whole world out there", he said. "It was more a problem of prioritizing your time, and knowing where is the best opportunity. It was really new stuff. It was really plowing new ground".

In 1970 Bryant asked him whether he'd like to be Dow's ag manager for Japan.5 Again he said yes. "We enjoyed that move", Hagaman said.   "I think the whole family liked Japan. We look back on it with a lot of pleasure. I liked the work. I liked the Japanese".

"I saw working with the Japanese as easy and rewarding", he said. "In my opinion, a Japanese respects a foreigner who comes in and tries to understand their culture, but what they don't respect is a foreigner who steps over that line and tries to become a Japanese. It's a balance. It's going far enough to try to understand while maintaining your own identity, but not going so far as to make an attempt to become Japanese, because they see that as sacrificing your own identity. A person who sacrifices his own identity has no respect among the Japanese..."

Hagaman made a serious study of the Japanese language while he was working the ag beat in Japan. "I had a tutor", he said. "I had a tutor most of the time I was there. I just gradually got a little better. I'd probably take two or three hours of lessons a week. I lived in Yokohama and I'd study it on the train going back and forth. I would certainly not say it was a serious effort. I never attempted or even got remotely close to a business discussion in Japanese. My objective was to be not dependent so I could function, I could go to stores and buy things and travel and stay in hotels and eat in restaurants, and that sort of thing where no English was spoken, and be functional. That was my objective, and I accomplished that objective. "

"It's hard to say you are really friends with very many Japanese", Hagaman said. "In all my time in either living or traveling to Japan I can say that I really have one true Japanese friend. We'd done business with them. He's with a major trading house, and has a very good chance of becoming the next president of this house. I've now known him for 25-plus years, and we see each other occasionally. Over time we got to be pretty good friends. I saw him maybe six or eight months ago. We were talking about old times and about being good friends. We were riding in a car, and he said to me, 'I'm glad that we met when we did and became good friends when we did'. Something like that. I said, 'What do you mean?' He looked at me like, how dumb can you get, and he said, 'Because if we met today there wouldn't be enough time'. There's not 25 years left. It's just very simple. In his culture he has to know somebody for that long and have enough experiences before he could classify that person (as a friend). As far as he's concerned, he's got all the friends he's ever going to have, because there flat out just isn't enough time left to make any more. That gives you some insight into how a Japanese thinks".

In 1973, after six years in the Orient, the Hagamans returned to the U.S., where he took on an assignment as the product manager for animal nutrition products, consisting mainly of Kedlor. He was home barely a year when he was asked to go back to the Pacific again. "I think they were looking for somebody with some experience there", he said. "They knew I liked the Pacific. They came and asked me if I wanted to go back, and I said, 'Yes'". He became business development manager for ag in the Pacific basin. Pharmaceuticals were added to his portfolio in 1976.

"We ran the business mainly through business teams", Hagaman said. Anthony Lee Hok Lang, product marketing manager for insecticides and miticides, for example, was chairman of the Dursban and Reldan (an analog of Dursban) team. Other members of that team came from New Zealand and Indonesia. M. C. Foong, product manager for grasskillers, was chairman of the Dowpon products team, with James C. Karl, manager of the Dowpon plant at Medan, in northeast Sumatra. Michael D. Campbell, marketing manager for broadleaf herbicides, was chairman of the broadleaf herbicides team, with the production manager of the plant at New Plymouth, New Zealand, and Barbara J. Furches, formulation research chemist.

"Dow utilized business teams earlier than most companies", Hagaman said, most of them in the Pacific organized by Lee F. Dupuy, a retired U.S. Army officer who became Dow's vice president for business development in the far East .

"We always tended to focus teams on what they could do", Hagaman said. "I don't think it makes a lot of sense to get a group together from Japan and Australia and Asia and say, 'How are we going to develop this product?' They are miles apart. But to get a group together and say, 'How are we going to do this in Japan?' Or to get another group together and say, 'How are we going to do this for Asia?' That makes a lot of sense, and I think that works pretty well. That's kind of what we did. We tried to build fences around the teams too, so they didn't get too far afield, and tried to keep them focused on manageable issues".

Two years later Hagaman's life changed completely. He was named executive vice president and general manager of the Korea Pacific Chemical Corporation, in Seoul, Korea, owned jointly by Dow and the Korean government. Dupuy was the president. Hagaman and his family moved to Korea, where they spent the next five years, with Hagaman eventually becoming Dow's regional manager for Korea. He returned to the Ag business and to the U.S. only in 1983, when Dow pulled out of Korea after a stiff dispute with the Korean government.6

He returned to Midland as corporate product director for Ag in Dow's Corporate Product Department, assuming the responsibility for global product direction of commercial agricultural products. There he worked closely with John Lillich. "I handled the commercial products and he handled the new products", Hagaman said. "We worked side by side". A little later he was promoted to vice president of Dow Chemical USA and general manager of North American ag products. "I was only in that job for a year", he said. "I just kind of got my feet on the ground with it, and then I took over the global ag responsibility in December, 1985".

That set the stage for the consolidations that occurred in later years.

In the spring of 1986 Hagaman formed an Agricultural Biotechnology Review Board, to provide strategic direction for Dow research and business activities in the fast-developing field of agricultural biotechnology. "I think that we knew then, and we still know today, that biotechnology is going to have an impact on the agricultural chemical business", he said. "When that's going to happen and how it's going to happen is a lot less clear. That was our first attempt to really look at biotechnology. It resulted in us buying United AgriSeeds Inc. It resulted in us establishing our plant genetics research program. We currently (1992) spend about 20 percent of our discovery research budget in biotechnology. Biotechnology is going to have an impact. It's less clear to what extent and how quickly, but it is going to have an impact".7

By the time Hagaman retired, in 1997, DowElanco sales had reached $2.175 billion. That was also the year that Dow bought out Eli Lilly, and the firm, now owned entirely by Dow, was retitled Dow AgroSciences, Dow Agro for short.

"John has a much greater intellect than most people might see at first impression", Fischer said. "He is a very deep thinker with a great mind. He knows the ag business probably as well or better than anybody in the industry, even today, and he was a great guy to follow".

Charles Fischer

Chapter 16

Charlie Fischer and Globalization

Charlie Fischer grew up in a little farmhouse in the outback of Texas, about 80 miles south of Austin, with his parents and three brothers. The place had no electricity and no running water, and his mother carried well water up a hill.

"But my Mom" he said, "was determined to get us all educated. Four boys all graduated from college with a father that never made a hundred dollars a week".1

He had an uncle who was a Ford dealer in the nearby town of Cuero, where he went to high school, and in the summers he "started working with my cousins who were selling the cars. I started selling cars and sold them all the way through college. My senior year in college, I think I sold 25 cars to my classmates. I started to realize that basically I was a salesman. I liked to sell and I liked the people relationship".

"Athletics was also a good experience", he said, "learning teamwork. We'd ride our bicycles into town and play on the organized teams. I played baseball from February 15 to August 1 every year. I played football. I always wanted to be in charge so I tried to be the quarterback. Small and slow doesn't make you a star, but determination got me on the team anyway. I look back and say that I always wanted to be in charge. I wanted to be the leader of the school. I wanted to be the leader of the team. I wanted to be the leader of what I did at Dow. It's kind of been throughout my life that I liked to be up front".

While he was still in junior high school he built a caged chicken house from a blueprint. "I had about 270 laying hens", he said. "The eggs rolled out and everything. I hired my brothers to help me clean the eggs every night. We cleaned eggs on the kitchen table every night for years, to get them ready for sale...The joke in the family is that I had all the ideas, but I hired my brothers to do all of the work, which is not exactly true, but they like to say it that way".

He graduated from Texas A & M University in 1964 with a degree in dairy science, just as the war in Vietnam was heating up, and immediately went into the army. "My artillery battalion was the only artillery battalion at Fort Sill (Oklahoma) that did not go to Vietnam, en masse", he said. "So I did not go to Vietnam although I stayed at Fort Sill and trained many, many people that did go to Vietnam".

Hillard L. Smith, famous among the aggies as a recruiter --- he was also for many years manager of herbicide sales -- came to Texas A & M and talked to Fischer about joining the Dow aggies. "I didn't pick Dow", he said. "Dow just happened to be on campus and (I thought) yes, I'll go and see them....he offered me a trip to Midland. I came in January of 1966, and I never thought I would live in Midland, Michigan, so I didn't even look at the fact that there were snow banks higher than my head".

As his first assignment, Dow sent him to Lubbock, Texas, to participate in a nematode project. "My job was to call on farmers and ask them if I could take soil samples from their cotton fields", he recalled. "I would take (the samples) to a Texas A & M laboratory in Lubbock where they would be analyzed for nematode counts. Then, with that, we would try to convince them that if they had enough nematodes, they should use our product for control of those nematodes. Our product was called Fumazone, a product that later we had to take off the market because it was proved to reduce sperm counts in humans. Dibromochloropropane, DBCP, is what it was...I did that for two years and then I was offered a full field sales assignment".

He got a call one day "and they said, 'Charlie, we want you to move to Billings, Montana. Would you do that?' And I said, 'Of course I would do that. When do I go?' His territory was all of eastern Montana. The next summer he married his girl when she graduated from Texas Tech, not in Billings but in Boise, Idaho. He had been transferred to Boise, and his territory now included all of southern Idaho, all of Utah, part of Nevada, and half of Oregon, a very large territory,.

"But it has pockets", Fischer said. "Agriculture out there is in pockets, wherever the river goes and the water is available for irrigation is where the farming is. I was able to help the market grow in Telone which still, even today, is a very, very important product for Dow and Dow

AgroSciences. It's a by-product of epichlorohydrin production that we take and clean up. It's a great soil fumigant. Idaho was a great experience. The onion production in eastern Oregon was great. There were a lot of Japanese farmers. It was high input agriculture."

Soon he began to move up the advancement ladder. "In the early days, my ambition was not to run ag", he said. "I didn't know what that would even have meant, but I sure wanted to be a district sales manager. As soon as I got to be that, I wanted to be a group manager. I just wanted to keep my ambition moving with my success. And as soon as I understood what running all the ag business would be, I had the confidence that I would be able to do it. Whether I would be chosen to do it, I wasn't sure, but I certainly thought I had the ability to do it. It turned out I got that opportunity".

In his only detour from an agricultural focus he became product manager for organic chemicals. "At that time, ag was not only ag, it was ag organic. The basis behind that was that organic chemicals was struggling a lot in the early 1970s. It was one of those times when there was an oversupply of organic chemicals. At that time Bob Naegele was the head of ag and Frank Popoff 2 was the director of marketing for ag. Both of these guys were really not aggies. They were organics guys.   I was offered a job in ag. I went to see Frank, and I said, 'Frank, you know, I don't know if I want to take that job'. And he said, 'Well, what job do you want?' I said, 'I want to be a product manager in organics. I want to have a broadening of my experience'. He said, 'Okay'. I became the product manager for ethylene oxide and derivatives. Right at that time there was the biggest shortage of chemicals, in my history at least, and everybody wanted everything that we had. So it wasn't exactly that I had to sell it, it was more that I had to allocate it. I think the record would show that I was seen as having great success in that job.

"And then a guy who did have a lot of influence, Leo A. MacDonald, who had been an organics business manager, was named the director of marketing for ag. Leo had a great ambition to change Dow Ag into a force in the market that we had not really achieved before.

"In the early 1970s the ag market was really starting to roll. Companies like Ciba-Geigy, Bayer, and some names that are no longer around, many companies had really started to take great advantage of this growing market for agricultural products. Some revolutionary products had been invented, like trifluralin by Eli Lilly, atrazine by Ciba, and others that had great use in the Midwest corn and soybean market. Dow had taken the role of saying 'We're going to have a few people. We're not going to have a cast of thousands. We're going to sell it more like chemicals', and unfortunately, we missed out on some of the early growth. We were not aggressive enough in the early 1970s and the late 1960s to really take part in this revolution of agricultural products. We were good. We had good products, but we weren't on the leading edge.

"Well, Leo wanted to get us on the leading edge. I was ready then to move out of my product manager's job into a district manager's job, and he convinced me that I should come back to ag and be a district manager in Atlanta. I couldn't turn down Atlanta very easily. That sounded great. Eventually, whatever the company asked me to do, I normally did. So I went down there and did that."

He stayed in Atlanta for three years -- "the most fun job I ever had" , he called it -- and then was summoned back to Midland to be the product manager for industrial ag products. That included herbicides for range and pasture and lighting rights of way, all of the termite business, and the Dursban business for cockroaches.

"One thing I did in that job probably had the most significant impact long term", he said, "and it's one I've been fairly proud of doing. We had a product, 2,4-D phenoxy, that was a big product for Dow for many years. We had Formula 40 and Esteron 99 Concentrate that were almost like the birthright from the old pioneers of Dow. Those were it. We were trying to become a real force in the Midwest, and every time our sales reps would go to a customer they'd be trying to sell Lorsban and N-Serve and some of the new products, but they'd spend the whole time arguing about the price of 2,4-D and never get to Lorsban. We were selling it to one group of guys and competing with the same guys at the dealers. It was a mess.

"And I had an idea. I said, 'Look, let's not compete with our own customers. Let's figure out who our competitors are and let's position ourselves to compete against them and not our customers, and let's get out of this brand-name product fight'. We found a small company that wanted to get into the 2,4-D brand, so we worked out a deal where we sold them our brand and became a technical supplier to them and to all of our other customers and didn't compete with them in the market. It took all the pressure off our field reps, who didn't have to negotiate every day about the retail price of 2,4-D. I think we sold it for $25 million -- the brand name, with a supply contract, and so on -- and that has become a model of how to manage products in ag that have kind of passed their day. It really helped change Dow's approach to the market. It was seen over the years as a great success, and I felt good about that".

"When I came back to Midland the Dursban business was $12.5 million at Dow Agro. Eventually it became $150 million. Not all of that happened on my shift but I did have a lot of influence in getting us to put Dursban into the termite market", he said.

"At that time chlordane3 was the prominent and preferred product for termites, and it was a fantastic product and it was very inexpensive. But we knew that the EPA had some real problems with chlordane and were going to try to ban it. So we registered Dursban, at some expense, for termites. And then we lost it. Everybody said, 'You have to sell it for a lot less'. I said, 'No, we're not going to sell it for any less. We're going to sell it at a price that we can make a lot of money on it because we're not going to sell any until chlordane is gone anyway. We can't sell it cheap enough to beat chlordane. First of all, chlordane is a much better product for termites, but the EPA doesn't like it and what we have to do is provide an alternative'. And we did. Eventually it became around a $100 million (per annum) use of Dursban at a very nice margin. Unfortunately, I was also the guy who had to go to the EPA and voluntarily take the product off the market, about two years ago (i.e., in 2002).

"The EPA moves through phases", he said. "They were happy to have (Dursban) become a replacement for chlordane, but then when they had another replacement they were happy for Dursban to go, because of some issues they thought they had. So I saw Dursban rise and fall, but we made a lot of money with it."

For a time Dursban was the world's largest-selling insecticide. "Its high-water mark was probably when we hit $500 million (in annual sales)", he said. "It's probably now more like $250 million. It was the largest seller and still is a fantastic product. But things ebb and flow and there are new products that also have some great qualities that have taken some of its market. As I say, we 'volunteered' to take our product off the market. It's like you're going to the gas chamber and if you walk, you're volunteering. If they drag you, you're not, but nobody agreed that they really wanted to do this. So we just talked about it and decided to fight them further would not be of any value. I got hate letters about that, by the way, from people who are against agreeing with the government on anything. They would say, 'You're a traitor. You didn't fight for your rights'. I think if there are millions of lives at stake, we couldn't make that kind of judgment, but this was an economic question, and it didn't make any sense for us to fight it any further. So we volunteered to take it off the market".

Back in Midland he was assigned to the corporate product department, whose job was to coordinate Dow's businesses world-wide. "That is when I really got exposed to international agriculture, international Dow, and travel", he said.

One of his first assignments involved a trip to Japan. "We had a contract with a Japanese company by the name of Toray for a raw material", he said. "The contract lasted two or three more years for this raw material, and we wanted out of the contract. We wanted our partner to make the product. I was sent to Japan to negotiate us out of this contract. There are a couple of notable things about that. This was the first time I'd made an overseas trip anywhere. I land in Tokyo, which to this day is still the most foreign city I've ever been to, and in the early 1980s it was very foreign -- no road signs or letters that you could read. I had scribbled on a piece of paper how to get from the airport to my hotel in Japanese. After I rode the train, got on the bus, and give it to the taxi driver who got me there, I was afraid to go out of the hotel more than two blocks. I didn't think I could find my way back. Of course, I was experiencing jetlag for the first time, which was tough, and then I went into this meeting with these Japanese guys to negotiate out of this contract. We talked a lot but the sense of it was, 'Did you sign the contract?' 'Yes'. 'Don't you follow your contracts?' 'Well, normally'. 'Well, that's what we want to do'. That's it. End of conversation. Midland would hardly take that as an answer, but that was the answer. They signed a contract and that was what they were going to live by, and don't talk to us again until it's over. So I wasn't very successful on that trip. But it was my first opportunity to travel overseas. I loved it. I'd come home and I'd bring the camera and the geisha doll and my family started to like the idea about international life".

One day he got a call from Joe Downey, then the head of Dow agro, and he said, "Charlie, I really hate to do this, but I'm obligated to tell you that you're being offered a job". "Oh yeah", said Charlie, "what's that?" "The job as No. 1 ag man in Brazil that you turned down two years ago". Charlie said, "Okay, I'll go home and we'll talk about it". He went home "and my wife said, 'I think we ought to do it'. And I said, 'Okay, we're going to go'. Then I said, 'Joe, we want to go to Brazil'. He said, 'You will?' I said, 'Yes, we'll go'. So we went, and that started my true international experience".

"Brazil was a different world, and I have to say, in my family's experience, in my 38 years at Dow, that was probably one of the greatest times we had. When I tell people that I've been in Brazil and I lived in France, they say, 'Oh, you must have loved France'. I say, 'No, I loved Brazil. France was a great experience, but I loved Brazil'.

"You move into a city like Sao Paulo", he said, "and there's a lot of expats (expatriates) there; a lot of really interesting people from many companies -- Ford, GM, Caterpillar, and so on. So we had great friends. It was a stimulating environment. Sao Paulo is a city that you wouldn't want to visit, but it's a great place to live, great restaurants and a lot of good people to know, and the Brazilians are wonderful as far as wanting you to understand their community. They like Americans a lot. The downside to Brazil and Sao Paulo in particular is security. They generally weren't going to steal something from you and then shoot you. They're going to steal it and then give you two dollars for a cab ride. They were hungry. They wanted money for something they needed. But we were careful and never had an incident while we were there. We lived in a very nice apartment in a closed community and had a great, great three years.

"Business-wise, it's tough to do business in another language. The Brazilians were okay with English, but the business society was in Portuguese, whereas in Europe, pretty much the business community is English today. But there it's Portuguese, and I struggled to learn Portuguese. I speak Portuguese relatively well for social and eating and traveling, but to negotiate a business contract in Portuguese would not be something that I would trust myself to do, so I had Brazilian colleagues who helped me there, which was probably good too because they got the experience of working on business things. But that was a challenge. Ethics are a challenge. You've got to play the game very straight. You certainly have opportunities to play it other ways. There are lots of different approaches in some of the rest of the world than we have. But it was a good assignment. We had good success in the business. I very much liked the people that I worked with".

He learned some basic things about Brazilian agriculture. "I traveled in the northeast to papaya plantations where I learned about feudal agriculture", he said. "Even today the papaya plantations are owned by a rich family in Rio and managed by some professional manager, but the people are almost like serfs. It's pretty sad. Their education is minimal. The housing is very primitive. It's warm the year around so you can get away with that, but it was depressing. Even today a lot of the children in the northeast region, their minds don't develop because of poor nutrition, and I've seen many that just couldn't think very well. They didn't have the nutrition when they were children. So Brazil has its challenges, then and now. A lot of people who go to Brazil really, really hate the visibility of poverty. Even in a city like Sao Paulo, there are favelas -- slums-- and you see real poverty. I don't believe I'm cold-hearted, but growing up in the south in the United States, you see a little bit more of that than you might in Midland, Michigan, so I could accept that that's how it was, but it really was distasteful for many people. Brazil tries to do something about it, but it's a big challenge".

"Brazilian agriculture is doing extremely well", he said. "They have the capability of being as good as the United States in many crops, but certainly in soybeans hands down. They will beat the United States (in that crop) eventually. They can grow as good or better soybeans on a lot less expensive land, with less input, and their biggest challenge is to get the infrastructure of getting the crop to the markets. They are and will be more of a formidable competitor to U.S. soybeans in the future. They can also do corn and other things. The U.S. should not plant one stick of sugar cane or one sugar beet if you talk about pure economics. Politically, we will, because we protect our growers, but Brazil can grow sugar cheaper than we can even think about growing it and deliver it here with a quality that's as good as we can do. But politics is very much involved in agriculture, even today.

"I've traveled extensively in the orange area. Their orange juice plants are second to none, and there's no way a Florida orange can compete with a Brazilian orange. There's no way. You can adjust the acidity to make it like the Americans want to drink. You can't tell the difference. Again, we maintain some market here. They are the largest coffee grower. It's more the competitive coffee. They don't grow the high, high quality, but they grow good coffee. It's a great country, and I love South America and particularly, Brazil."

The biggest Dow product in Brazil at that time was Tordon herbicide. "Tordon is an herbicide that was really invented by Dow before its time", he said. "It's a product that a gram or two per acre is effective. Today that's a commonplace thing, to invent a product that a gram an acre is effective, but at that time it took usually two or three pounds an acre for it to be effective. So this was really a breakthrough product. Early on, we probably tried to take it into a few too many sophisticated crop areas, and residual was a problem, but in range and pasture it is a tremendous product for control of hard-to-kill weeds. Brazilians love the product. It's a product mixed with 2,4-D but extensive in improved pasture management.

"Some people say, 'Oh, they're spraying it over the jungles'. Well, let me guarantee you, none has been sprayed over the jungles for one very good reason: you can spray it today, spray it tomorrow, spray it next week, and you're never going to get the jungle knocked down to where you're getting grass.   Do we ever get it sprayed on places where the jungle was torn down and burned and made into grass? Yes, of course. But the truth is the vast majority of it is more in regions that are not Amazon rainforest areas. Those are very weak soils. They don't last. So they're more in high-quality pasture-land kind of applications. The weeds come, and this is used extensively in keeping the weeds and brush out of those pastures. It's a very big market.

"We have some products for sugar cane, such as a product called Tebuthiron. We've had a fairly big 2,4-D market for sugar cane and wheat. There is some wheat grown there. We do well with Lorsban and now spinosad. It's a very broad range. Just about every product that Dow makes gets sold in Brazil.

"Dow has a tradition of believing that 'if it's right, we go do it'", he said, "but I think we're more politically sensitive today. We have a product that could be used for the control of coca plants, and the U.S. government and Colombia were interested and were anxious to have us supply this product for spraying broadly in Colombia, as an herbicide that kills coca plants (cocaine is derived from the leaves of the coca plant)".

"But the risk for a company like ours is just too much. The U.S. government is great at getting you into it, but they're just not very good at helping you out of it. We knew that if we sprayed this product broadly in Colombia that there are a lot of subsistence gardens in these areas (the areas where the coca plant grows), and that we'd kill the heck out of them if we sprayed them. So we have really resisted that. The government would have too great odds. In the end, they can make you do whatever they want, but we're more cautious about that. Now, as a citizen who would like not to see coca products flowing into the United States (from Colombia), it is a tough thing. You want to be supportive of your government, but sometimes it's darn hard. It's darn hard. We as a company have to make them play it by the rules, which they can do. They can play it by the rules and give you the assurances. They don't like to, though. They really hate to do it. They would have to go so high in the government. But we as a company are much more careful about that today and we should be. I think we have to be. I think it's hard, when times are tough in a company, to keep your determination to be an open company and listen. Times have been tough for the last few years, and it's stressed us a little bit. Society has changed, and our responsibility to society".

Dealing with the EPA as a government agency was a "mixed" experience, Fischer said. "When you say the EPA, that's a big place", he said. "You have the political management, and they kind of trend with the administration. If you have a Democratic administration, you're likely to get a more liberal atmosphere. Maybe that's not the right word, exactly, but a person like Lynn Goldman was very, very conservative about any use of chemicals and would probably like to see them all gone. We had a lot of trouble with her. But when you get a Republican administration it's probably a little more, in our eyes, balanced, and we had some very good experience with the political people.

"Then, as in most bureaucracies, you have the bureaucrats, and there you get zealots for some cause or another, and they have a lot of power. They won't overrule a scientist within their organization; they can't do it. The lawyers in the EPA are very important. We've done well with them, but we did better as we became less confrontational and more willing to go through the tests. We're going to find out all we can find out about these products. We never have sold things that we thought were a risk or unsafe, but we have to be more open to other points of view about some of the science. Science is not perfect either, because we're humans working on it and we find out new things. But I'd say we do pretty well with the EPA, and today we're doing extremely well.

"One of the things we've decided is that we won't bring forward (to the EPA) things that they won't like. We know what they don't like, and we can argue all day about what they should like, but we know they won't like it. So we bring things that we think they will like".

"Today we have a product named spinosad. We sell it as Tracer or Success, but the common name is spinosad, and it's a product that's from a fermentation of bacteria. We take a by-product of that production and it's an insecticide. The EPA loves this product. It's a natural product. It's even approved for organic uses, if you don't put the wrong solvents in it. They spread it all over California for med fly and over organic gardens, and everybody is happy about it. The good thing is that it works, which is unusual for an organic kind of product. So they love that.4

"Then we found an analog of that, and from that we can make another insecticide. It's another spinosad, and the EPA is almost pushing this harder than we're willing to move to get the product on the market. The EPA, in spite of what some of (their critics) say, wants solutions. The farming community is trying to get them to register products. The environmental community is trying to stop them from doing it. And they play a tough battle in the middle. So they love things like (spinosad), and I think we really benefited by saying, 'we're going to bring things to the market that they like and want, and, of course, they have to work. If they don't work, forget it'. They'll register them, but you won't sell any, so you've got to have both.

"Steve Johnson, who is currently one of the number twos at the EPA, is a close colleague of mine. I have worked with him very closely on a number of issues. Not always do we agree or could he agree with us, but we've had a very good relationship. We can get in the door, that's for sure. I don't know the new EPA administrator, the governor from somewhere. But we'll try to get to know them and cooperate, but also push our point of view.

"I've worked a lot over these past few years with the government, a lot of congressmen, senators, and so on. That's an important part of a job in business today, having your political doors open. They won't always do what you want; but you can get your word in."

His plea was for balance. "I am a believer in balance", he said, "and do I think if there were not a Rachel Carson writing Silent Spring, would we be as far in our use of modern, more safe products?5 Probably not. (On the other hand), if we'd done everything Rachel Carson proposed forty years ago, or whenever it was, more people would not have had nutrition and would have died from disease and malnutrition, and so on. So a balance is good. It's my job to try to be a little more radical on one side. It's their job to be a little more radical on the other. Hopefully, in the end, we get what's best in the balance. I don't believe it's wrong that we have people who have a different opinion than mine, and I ask them not to belive that I'm wrong. But together we'll be more right. I don't know where the line is gong to be. I'll pull it this way and they'll pull it that way. But I think a balance is good in society, for all of us. That's why I guess I'm a moderate when it comes to many things".

His move from Brazil to France was quite unexpected. "I thought after four years in Brazil, and my family thought after four years in Brazil, that we'd be back in America and our kids would be finishing school here", he said, "so it was a big decision to move from one foreign country to another. A new language, different schools, not as good schools, in fact, for our kids -- but it was an opportunity for me, from one country and a relatively small business of $60 million yearly to probably at that time the most important region in ag in the Dow company, Europe. It was a great move for me. I somehow at this time coerced my wife into going. It was tough for my wife to go to France. It was just not as welcoming an international community".

They moved to Valbonne, France, about 10 miles north of Cannes and the French Riviera. "It was beautiful. We came to love it and enjoyed it. It was a great experience", he said.

"As a career move that was a tremendous move", he said. "We had all of Africa, all of Europe, all of the Soviet Union, the Middle East. It was very diverse. There were many opportunities. There were different political systems all over. It really helped me become a more complete, global business person".

A year or so after he arrived at Valbonne Dow and Eli Lilly decided they would merge their agricultural companies into a firm to be called DowElanco. A few months later he was informed he would be the manager of DowElanco in Europe. DowElanco became a free-standing company, and every part of the company was taken out of Dow and made into DowElanco. "We stayed at Valbonne but actually moved out of the Dow buildings into our own building there. We formed our own legal companies", he said.

"Some Dow people are not going to like to hear this, but my seven years in DowElanco was the most rewarding period in my whole career", he said. "I wish Dow would find a way to give more people the opportunity to run their own deal at some place other than at the very top. If they could pull more things apart and let them run their own deal, they'd have a lot more satisfied employees. It is so much fun.

"Now that's not to say you don't have responsibility. We had to answer to the (DowElanco) board, of which Dow had three members and Lilly had two, but on a daily basis we really could take it where we needed to go. I think because of that we formed a really competitive ag company. It's great to have the resources of Dow, and I've said again and again at meetings with Dow management that we have the best of both worlds versus some of our competitors.

"Some of our competitors are truly free-standing companies. We are a business unit within Dow that has been given the autonomy to be an ag company, with all the benefits of the resources of a $30 billion company like Dow. Those other companies can't have a treasury as competent as ours. They can't have an IT system as efficient and as successful as ours. Yet we can be just as product- and market-focused as they can. So it's a great combination if Dow continues to find the balance of not trying to micromanage the aggies on ag issues and being very, very dominant in the functions that serve the ag business, like treasury.

"When Dow gets going really good it will just make ag look tiny and that would be great", he said. "But I'll tell you, the cash flow of Dow Agroscience last year made a huge impact on Dow and it will again this year, but it was particularly important last year. Dow would not have come close to making its dividend last year without ag. Dow knows it, and that's good. That's what we should do. That's what we were put there to do. But it was very critical. We've tried to merge ag. We've tried a lot of things with ag. But I think ag is a very good partner in a company that wants to have some more specialized markets and today still has to go through these big cycles that we have to go through".

Fischer became president and CEO of Dow Agrosciences on March 1, 1999, when John Hagaman retired.6

In the middle nineties he had an experience that left him eternally grateful to the Dow company. "My wife became ill with cancer", he said, "and over the period of half of 1994 through to February of 1997 she got progressively, progressively worse. It was not only a terminal cancer, it was a very difficult cancer, where she lost her tongue and eventually she didn't eat or talk for the last two years. I'm not saying that for sympathy, but I really want to compliment Dow because I was allowed to do my job - - a very important job in Dow -- in a way that I could also be a committed husband who needed to be away a lot with my wife. We were in Indiana some, we were in Chicago. We were in a lot of places. We used the Dow plane to fly my staff to Houston to have a meeting with me because I couldn't leave. It really allowed me to have a career at the same time I was a husband. I was interviewed by the head hunters who actually helped decide whether I was going to be the new president of Dow Agro. I felt that I had shown my character by being able to do both, but I also believe very strongly that Dow showed character by allowing me to do that. Eventually I got to be the president, even though I had been a part-time employee for a couple of years. I guess sometimes you think, well, I had a job high enough that the president knew me and of course I should expect good treatment, but I always try to make sure that any employee gets the same fair chance to work through difficult situations. That maybe helped me be a better employee in a way. I don't want to re-live it by any means, but it showed some great character on the company's part, and hopefully I lived up to their expectations on my side.

"So that was a very difficult and important part of my life. Hopefully I don't have to live through that again, but in every phase of your life there are challenges and benefits. I probably became more in love with my wife then than I ever had, but yet I was still able to meet my eventual career goal of being head of ag. I did that for five years and then it was time for me to move on and play more golf".

There is more to the story. "I've now remarried", Fischer said. "This is a funny little story because after I'd been single for a while I'd jokingly say, I'm so happy that if this had to happen that I didn't live in Midland, Michigan, because how would I ever find a new mate in Midland, because there are just not enough people there. I was a single guy there once, 35 years ago, but now it would really be tough. I had lots of opportunities to meet ladies in Indianapolis, but then I was introduced to a a lady in Midland, Michigan, and I married her. So maybe you shouldn't pre-judge too early. Andrew Liveris introduced me to my current wife, and somewhat unfortunately she couldn't move to Indianapolis because of her children.7 The court wouldn't allow them to, so I've been commuting for three years and that's been another challenge. But I've managed it and it was a good three years. Now I'm in the process of moving to Midland, Michigan, because I have retired and I look forward to living there".

"In August of 2003, as I was turning 61, "Fischer said, "I was thinking. Dow Agrosciences is going to have one tremendous year in 2003, and it's really in the bag. It's done. There's nothing I can do to stop it or make it any better, particularly. It's done. So therefore, the president of Dow AgroSciences ought to be spending his or her time thinking about how to draw the next line in the sand about where we're going to take this company next. We set an audacious goal. We're going to make it. What are we going to do next? Then start writing up all the ways and think about all the ways we're going to make it happen. That's going to take a person full-time, enthusiastic, and it will probably take two or three years to do something really, really significantly better than we're going to do this year. Do I, Charlie Fischer, want to commit myself to that kind of intensity for another three years? I said, 'I don't think so'. And, in fact, I don't even know that Dow wants me to do that because there's a time when the new generation needs to come in and start going. I've got some great guys who can do this job very well. I don't know that I want to be that intense in my job for the next three or four years, and I think it's probably time for me to go.

"The thing about Dow Agro or any company like that, is you can't go half-speed. You just can't, because the day you go half-speed, someone will call you up with a respectable question and you've got to have an answer. I didn't want to be that intense anymore,. So I thought it was time for me to change".

A few weeks later he retired and was succeeded as president of Dow Agrosciences by one of his lieutenants, Jerome Peribere, a Frenchman.

An Epilogue

And what about the future?

By the year 2050, we are told, the world's population will have risen to 11 billion persons, meaning, according to at least one expert observer, that "agriculture will have to produce more in one year than we've had to produce in our entire 12,000-year history".1

That will not be easy. In spite of their spectacular accomplishments of the 20th century, the aggies at Dow and elsewhere will be hard pressed to keep up with such a demand. Scientists everywhere will keep on looking for the pesticides and herbicides and fungicides of tomorrow, even though the bar is continually being raised for the registration of such new materials, which has become ever more difficult. The National Agricultural Chemicals Association says that nowadays, "to ensure that a product, when used properly, will not present any health or environmental concerns, it is subjected to more than 120 separate tests".2 It cannot fail any of them. If it does it will not make it to market. And some of these tests take years of field use and development to accomplish. In consequence, it is easy to see that the costs of introducing new products will continue to climb higher and higher, perhaps prohibitively so. Not many private firms will be able to shoulder the enormous long-term burden of discovering and bringing new products to market, and for the smaller firm it will become a total impossibility. And even then, failure of a proposed new product at one of the final hurdles on its route to the market, by which time that potential product represents an enormous investment, could well turn out to be disastrous for the firm that followed that route -- possibly even a shortcut to its bankruptcy.

But the future is hardly that gloomy. Fortunately for us, the successes of U. S. agriculture are well known. With less than seven per cent of the world's land, and less than one per cent of the world's farmers and farmworkers, the United States produces about half of the world's soybeans, 40 per cent of the corn, and a quarter of the beef and grain sorghum, according to former U.S. secretary of agriculture Mike Espy. The numbers for other crops are just as impressive. "American agriculture's story is truly one of unparalleled productivity and promise". 3

In fact, for a great American success story you need look no farther than American agriculture. In 40 years , corn yields, to cite one example, have more than tripled, from an average yield of 40 bushels per acre in 1952, 96 bushels in 1972, and 131.4 bushels in 1992, even though in that 40 years the area devoted to corn dropped about 10 per cent, from 81 million acres of corn in 1952 to 72.1 million acres of corn in 1992.

Where do Dow AgroSciences and the Dow aggies fit into this picture? The megamergers that have been occurring in the agricultural chemical field are not yet completed, in the opinion of Charlie Fischer. "If you look at the genesis (of the present situation), it's the need for more size to spend the money on research", he said. "It's pharmaceutical companies owning ag businesses that they don't want any more. There are three or four or five where that's been the case. It's those things and the desire to have more critical mass in the market. Some of those that have not been successful probably never will be.   So Dow has a decision to make, whether they want to get rid of us or try to make a stand with a smaller, yet very efficient company. We are the most efficient ag company in the market. Of the big players, we are the most efficient ag company in the market. We have lesser expense to sales than anybody by a lot. Through the benefit of using Dow as our resource on many things, it's really efficient".

The biggest such firms in the world today are Bayer and Syngenta. Bayer, Fischer said, is the result of mergers with Aventis, AgrEvo, and Hoechst "All of that family are now one", he said. "They're the largest. They have some work to do. They're still struggling to get through the mergers".

Syngenta, second largest, is a merger of Ciba-Geigy, Rhone-Poulenc, and Zeneca, "which was old ICI" (that is, the agricultural arm of ICI, the largest British chemical firm, Imperial Chemical Industries, Ltd.). "I would say they're the most capable company today", he said.

"Then you get to Monsanto, and Monsanto is still one of the biggest profit makers, with Roundup and their new biotechnology. If you ask for the leader in biotechnology, it's Monsanto, hands down..   Leagues ahead of everyone else.   Then it may be us or Syngenta on biotech".

Next in line is Dupont, "although Dupont has Pioneer Seeds, and if you put Pioneer Seeds with their business then they become a fairly big player". Dupont "spent $11 billion on Pioneer Seed", Fischer pointed out. "They're moving now toward food-related biotech, maybe with some success".

Dow AgroSciences is sixth on the list in sales volume, but tops in earnings. "In 2003 we made more money, absolutely, than anybody except one", Fischer said, "that being Syngenta. We made more money than all the rest of them. We were just way ahead of anybody else in productivity, dollars of revenue, in profit per dollar of sales. We have every right to be proud as a company of what ag is doing. The question, again and again, is, are we big enough to remain competitive in a very research-intensive market? Also a question that has to be asked is, is there good enough return on research in a very, relatively satisfied market? If the weeds are all dead, can you invent another herbicide that will be better? It's not as easy to do as it might have been thirty years ago.

"On the other side, I can argue that spinosad is showing (us) that (if and when) you get a new thought, a new insecticide that's really good, it's very, very successful.. Now, I believe that if Dow is going to stop doing aggressive research in ag, what they really ought to do is sell it, because if you don't do aggressive research, it's just a small commodity product company then. Why don't you just go to a big commodity product?"

Whatever the future may hold, the aggies will stick together. They seem to have closer, firmer bonds with each other than the ordinary run of mortals. They keep track of each other for many years after they've retired. They travel long miles for reunions with their former colleagues and co-workers. Is this because they've gone through crisis upon crisis together? Perhaps. Is it because they've had considerable success as a team together and have developed a stronger team spirit? Perhaps. Is it because they have shared a kindred sense of mission and have worked together for long years in pursuit of that mission? Is it related to the genuine satisfaction that comes with solving some of the basic problems of providing food for the masses? These all seem strong possibilities.

For whatever reasons, the aggies stick together.

FOOTNOTES

Prologue

1. See "Paris Green to Green Revolution -- The evolution of agricultural chemicals has a long, colorful history", by Denis Hayley, and "Curbing Crop Woes -- Fungicides, the foundation for disease control, play a large role in crop production and preservation", by H. Edwin Carley, both in Farm Chemicals magazine, 100th anniversary issue, September 1994.

2. Figures taken from "The Use and Significance of Pesticides in the Environment", by F. L. McEwen and G. R. Stephenson, John Wiley & Sons, Inc., New York, 1979

3. Millennium Year by Year, A Chronicle of World History from AD 1000 to the End of 1999, 2000 Edition, 1921.

4. Ibid., 1907.

5. Ibid., 1878, 1879.

6. "Poor Can't Afford Food in Niger", by Nafi Diouf, Associated Press, August 3, 2005, Detroit News; "Delay killing Niger's Children", by Michael Weiss, N.Y. Times News Service, August 5, 2005, Midland (Mi.) Daily News.

7. New Collegiate Dictionary.

8. Data from "The Food in Your Future -- Steps to Abundance", by Keith C. Barrons, Van Nostrand Reinhold Co., New York, 1975

9. Ibid.

10. "Nearly half a billion people get malaria each year. More than a million die. After decades of neglect, the world is renewing its fight against the disease". See "Malaria -- Stopping a Global Killer" , by

Michael Finkel, Photographs by John Stanmeyer, in National Geographic magazine, July 2007.

11. The EPA came into being on December 2, 1970, created by President Richard Nixon as part of a reorganization to unify federal environmental activities. William D. Ruckelshaus was the first administrator. At its inauguration EPA had 5,000 employees and a $1.3 billion budget.

Chapter 1

1. For history and details of these orchards and grounds, see "The Pines: 100 Years of the Herbert H. and Grace A. Dow Homestead, Orchards, and Gardens", by Tawny Ryan Nelb, published by the Herbert H. and Grace A. Dow Foundation, Midland, MI, 1999.

2. See, for example, H. H. Dow to The Rural New Yorker, New York City, April 1, 1907.

3. See "Chemistry, Congress, and Safe Foods", by Ken Reese, Today's Chemist at Work, Jan. 1994.

4. "Harvey W. Wiley -- An Autobiography", Bobbs-Merrill Co., Indianapolis, IN, 1930.

5. Herbert Dow stated his views on this subject fully in "Benzoate Sprays for Fruit Trees", published in the Midland Republican, April 10, 1908.

6. H. H. Dow to H. J. Wheeler, July 18, 1906; H. J. Wheeler to H. H. Dow, July 31, 1906.

7. Ibid.

8. H. H. Dow to Luther Burbank, Santa Rosa, Calif., August 1, 1906.

9. G. W. Carver to H. H. Dow, August 25, 1906 and March 27, 1907; Rupert E. Paris. to Carver, March 22, 1907.

10. "May Bar Benzoate of Soda", New York Commercial, July 14, 1908.

11. H. H. Dow to H. E. Hackenberg, Cleveland, July 18, 1908.

12. For an account of the Kettering-Midgley visits to Midland and their consequences, see E. N. Brandt, Growth Company, pp. 235-239.

13. Citations taken from Herbert H. Dow, Garden Book No. 3, 1918-1930, at Post Street Archives.

Chapter 2

1. This chapter is based mainly on the Papers of William J. Hale, focusing on his associations with the Dow Chemical Company and the Dow family, at the Post Street Archives in Midland. A second collection of Hale's Papers, including the records of his business ventures, is held at the Michigan State University Archives and Historical Collections, E. Lansing, MI

2. See "The Dizzy Dean of Chemistry", in Brandt, Growth Company, pp. 121-126.

3. Ibid, p. 124.

4. Ibid, p. 137.

5. Records of the Verdurin Co., Papers of William J. Hale, Michigan State University Archives.

6. Oral History, Ruth Hale Buchanan, June 13, 1991.

7. U.S. Patent 1,607,618, 1926, William J. Hale and Edgar C. Britton.

8. For history of the chemurgic movement, see Christy Borth, Pioneers of Plenty (Indianapolis and New York, Bobbs-Merrill Co., 1939.

9. "Farming Must Become a Chemical Industry", Dearborn (MI) Independent, Oct. 2, 1926.

10. "The Farm Chemurgic: Farmward the Star of Destiny Lights Our Way", by William J. Hale, The Stratford Co., Boston, Mass., 1934

11. See "Waste Not, Want Not: The Michigan Roots of the Farm Chemurgic Movement", by David E. Wright, Michigan History, Sept.-Oct. 1989, and "Historical Perspectives on the Farm Chemurgic Movement: Leo M. Christensen, Power Alcohol, and Chemurgic Entrepreneurship in the 1930s", David E. Wright, paper presented before American Association of Cereal Chemists, Miami, FL, Oct. 4, 1993.

See also, David E. Wright, "Alcohol Wrecks a Marriage: The Farm Chemurgic Movement and the USDA in the Alcohol Fuels Campaign in the Spring of 1933", in Agricultural History, Vol. 67, No. 1, Winter 1993.

12. Haynes, Williams. 1954. American Chemical Industry: A History. 6 Vols. New York. Reinhold.

13. Figures from "Milk cost kicked up by rush to ethanol", by Alejandro Bodipo-Memba, Detroit Free Press, June 24, 2007.

14. Oral History, Bonnie B. Matheson, June 7, 2005.

Chapter 3

1. Much of this chapter is drawn from Oral History, Donald Sanford, interview by the author, Oct. 13, 1984, at Brighton, Colorado. Sanford was 88 years old at the time of this interview. In connection with the references to Lee Doan, it should be noted that Leland I. (Lee) Doan, who had married one of Herbert H. Dow's daughters (Ruth) while both were students at the University of Michigan in 1916, in 1949 became president and CEO of The Dow Chemical Company, serving in that capacity until his retirement in 1960.

2. Gilbert A. Currie, a former Congressman, was a neighbor and friend of Don Sanford's father at Smiths Crossing, Michigan. Earl W. Bennett, treasurer of the Dow company at the time Sanford arrived, later became chairman of the board of the company
(1935), and served in that capacity until he retired in 1960.

3. W. R. Veazey was a faculty member at Case Institute of Technology in Cleveland who spent his summers for many years doing research at Dow in Midland. Later he became a member of the company's board of

directors and a full-time Dow employee and was involved in the research that led to many of the company's key products.

Chapter 4

1. See, for example, Will D. Carpenter, "Weed Whackers: Weed Control Comes of Age", in Farm Chemicals, 100th Anniversary edition, Sept. 1994.

2. Charles L. Hamner and H. B. Tukey, The Herbicidal Action of 2,4 Dichlorophenoxyacetic and 2,4,5 Trichlorophenoxyacetic Acid on Bindweed, Science, Vol. 100, No. 2590, Aug. 18, 1944, Pp. 154-155.

3. This chapter is based primarily on the Keith C. Barrons Papers, housed at the Post Street Archives in Midland, Michigan. See "The Phenoxy Herbicides Take Off", File 1-17 of these papers, and "The Dowpon Story", File 1-34.

4. Chemically MCPA is 2-methyl, 4-chlorophenoxyacetic acid.

5. Chemically silvex is 2,4,5-phenoxypropionic acid. Dalapon is 2,2-dichloropropionic acid.

6. File 1-34 "The Dowpon Story" and File 3-80, "Dalapon", Barrons Papers.

7. E. H. Blair to J. E. Johnson, "Proposal for Promotion of Dr. Keith C. Barrons to Development Scientist", Sept. 23, 1969 (Post St. Archives).

8. "A balanced overview of the pesticide controversy", Prof. James E. Dewey, professor of entomology at Cornell University and head of the chemicals/pesticides program at New York State College of Agriculture, in C&EN, Mar. 1, 1982

9. Are Pesticides Really Necessary? Keith C. Barrons, Regnery Gateway, Inc., Chicago, 1981.

10. Ibid, p. 89.

11. The Food in your Future, K. C. Barrons, Van Nostrand Reinhold Co., New York, 1975.
  Citation from "Organic Farming, The Whole Story", one of a series of pamphlets issued by Natiional Council for Environmental Balance, Inc., Louisville, KY, 1989.

12. A Catastrophe in the Making, With Letters to the Pope, An Agriculturist Tells Why Third World Population Growth Must Come Down, K. C. Barrons, Mancorp Publishing, Inc., Tampa, Florida, 1991.

13. Obituary, Keith Converse Barrons, Midland Daily News, Mar. 18, 2003.

Chapter 5

1. Dow Research Pioneers, 1888-1946, pp. 496 et seq.

2. Much of this chapter is drawn from Oral History, Robert D. (Barney) Barnard, interview by James C. Mackey, Feb. 21, 1989, at Walnut Creek, California.

3. "Okies" refers to the Oklahoma refugees who migrated in great numbers from Oklahoma to California during the "dust bowl" phenomenon in the Oklahoma area during the 1930's.

4. See "Wizard of the West", pp. 160-165, in Growth Company, by E. N. Brandt, 1997.

5. See "Vikane", among other sections of Dow in the West, 1976, and Oral History Clifford F. Thompson, Sept. 11, 2001.

Chapter 6

1. Resolution of the Senate Rules Committee, by Senator John A. Nejedly, California Legislature, "Relative to commending Dr. John F. Kagy for his outstanding contributions to California agriculture", Senate Rules Resolution No. 280 adopted May 1, 1972.

2. Much of this chapter is drawn from "Dow's Agricultural Research in Plant Sciences in the Western United States -- An Historical Sketch", by J. F. Kagy, "a short history of Agricultural Research as conducted in the Western Division of the Company from about 1941 to about 1972", an addendum to this paper entitled "Agricultural-Organic Research, Walnut Creek, Calif., 1964-1976", by C. R. (Dick) Youngson, and a second addendum, "History of the Dow-Davis Field Station", by L. E. (Jack) Warren, Dow Chemical Laboratory Report GS-1561, May 12, 1978.

3. Ibid.

4. DN (active ingredient) is 2-cyclohexyl-4,6-dinitrophenol.

5. The red citrus spider mite is Panonychus citri, McGregor. See also page 478 of Robert S. Karpiuk, "Dow Research Pioneers, 1888-1949". The materials furnished were 2-alkyl-4,6-dinitrophenols.

6. Op. cit., 2 above.

7. The active ingredient of Fumazone is 1, 2-dibromo--3-chloropropane.

8. The active ingredient of Nellite is N,N'-dimethyl phenylester of phosphorodiamidic acid.

9. Oral History, Julius E. Johnson, Sept. 9, 1988.

10. Business and Science, Dow Diamond, October 1950, "John F. Kagy"; and "Portrait of a Professional", The Bear Facts, publication of the Western Division, The Dow Chemical Company, 1972.

Chapter 7

1. Much of this chapter is taken from Oral History, Eugene Ellis Kenaga, an interview by James J. Bohning and the author in Midland, May 26, 1994.

2. See "The Story of M & T Chemicals, Inc.", by Roy A. Duffus, Jr., Codella Duffus Baker, Inc., New York, N.Y., 1965.

3. Lorsban is the trademark name for agricultural uses of chlorpyrifos; Dursban is the trademark name for household and aquatic uses of chlorpyrifos.

4. See "A Historical Account of Dow's Environmental Stewardship", by Eugene E. Kenaga, in Chemicals, Human Health, and the Environment, a Dow publication, 1977

Chapter 8

1. Silent Spring, by Rachel Carson, Houghton Mifflin Co., Boston, 1962

2.. For a fuller account of the dioxin controversy, see Growth Company, by E. N. Brandt, pp. 362-367.

3. "Effects of 2,4,5-T on Man and the Environment", Hearings Before the Subcommittee on Energy, Natural Resources, and the Environment, April 7, 15, 1970, Serial 91-60, pp. 375-376.

4. The principal source for this chapter is Oral History, Etcyl H. Blair, interview by E. N. Brandt and James J. Bohning, May 24, 1994, Post Street Archives.

5. "Chlorodioxins -- Origin and Fate", Etcyl H. Blair, editor, Advances in Chemistry Series 120, American Chemical Society, 1973, a symposium sponsored by the Division of Pesticide Chemistry at the 162nd Meeting of the ACS, Washington, D.C., Sept. 16-17, 1971.

6. E. H. Blair, Personnel File, Post St. Archives.

7. Oral History, E. H. Blair, op. cit..

Chapter 9

1. Much of this chapter is drawn from Oral History, Raymond H. Rigterink, interview by James J. Bohning and E. N. Brandt, Oct. 20, 1999, at Midland, Michigan.

2. For a more detailed description of the K-List, see pp. 428-429, Dow Research Pioneers, 1888-1946, or Chapter 5, "The K-List", of this volume.

3. Heterocyclic -- "designating a closed-ring structure, usually of either 5 or 6 members, in which one or more of the atoms in the ring is an element other than carbon, e.g., sulfur, nitrogen, etc. Examples are pyridine, pyrrole, furan, thiophene and purine" -- The Condensed Chemical Dictionary, 1981.

4. Oral History, Etcyl H. Blair, May 24, 1994. "Beilstein" refers to Friedrich Konrad Beilstein's Handbuch der organischen Chemie, a basic reference work for organic chemists. When Beilstein first published his handbook in 1881 it covered 1,500 compounds. The most recent printed edition, in 1998, covers more than seven million compounds, and it continues to expand online.

5. Zeneca Agricultural Products is the basic producer of Dacthal.

Chapter 10

1. Fletcher, like Ludwig, had earned a master's degree at Ohio State.

2. Much of this chapter is based on Oral History, Paul D. Ludwig, by James J. Bohning and E. N. Brandt, Midland, Michigan, June 10, 2004.

3. "Dow Agricultural Research in Texas Under Dr. Colby", in Oil, Paint & Drug Reporter, July 20, 1953.

4. Amprolium, a coccidiostat used in veterinary medicine, is 1-[(4-Amino-2-propyl-5-pyrimidinyl)-methyl]-2-picolinium chloride.

5. The book referred to is "The Seed from the East", by Bertha Holt and David Wisner, Los Angeles: Oxford Press, 1956.

Chapter 11

1. The main source for this chapter is Oral History, Cleve A. I. Goring, interview by the author, August 25, 2005. All quotes in chapter are taken from this interview unless otherwise indicated

2. Chemically, N-Serve is 2-chloro-6-trichloromethyl pyridine.
See also "How N-Serve Was Discovered" , K. C. Barrons Papers, File 3-81.

3. "ACS Heroes of Chemistry Award Honors Seven Dow Ag Veterans" , in Around Dow, a Dow Chemical Company publication, Sept.-Oct. 1999

4. Organic Chemicals in the Soil Environment, in 2 vols., edited by Cleve A. I. Goring and John W. Hamaker, Marcel Dekker, Inc., New York, 1972.

Chapter 12

1. Oral History, John Hunter Davidson, interviewed by the author, June 25, 2002, at Midland, Michigan. Much of this chapter is based on this document. For biographical data re Davidson see also Who's Who in America, 2000 Edition, and Patrol Craft Sailors Association, member biographies, "Too Good to Be Forgotten", circa 1990.

2. This was the basic patent covering Dinitro-ortho-cyclo-hexyl-phenol, the basis of an extensive series of agricultural products produced by The Dow Chemical Company. These products are sometimes referred to as "DN" products, as "Dinitro" products, or as DNOCHP products.

3. "Dow in Agriculture", No. 2 of a series, "Chemicals Indispensable to Industry", in the Dow Diamond magazine, a company publication, Vol. 3, No. 3, April 1940.

4. Oral History, J. H. Davidson, op. cit..

5. Silvex was discontinued in 1984, by EPA order, during dioxin investigations.
"Mid-20th Century Progress", in K. C. Barrons papers, 1-11; "Plant Growth Regulators", 2-54; and Chapter 12, "Growth Regulators", 3-83.

6. Transcript, 50th anniversary celebration of 2,4-D, by Dow AgroSciences, March 9, 1998, Midland, Michigan, pp. 27-28.

7. Oral History, A. Charles Fischer, June 8, 2004, Midland, Michigan.

Chapter 13

1. Eulogy, Jack C. Little, at funeral of Howard Johnston, April 23, 1999, at Heather Farm Garden Center, Walnut Creek, Calif.

2. "Epitaph, Howard Johnston", by Joan Morris, staff writer, Walnut Creek (Calif.) Times, April 22, 1999.

3. Ibid.

4. "The Origin and Development of the Chemistry of Halogenated Pyridines in the Western Division", by Howard Johnston, Western Division, The Dow Chemical Company, November 1989 (in the Post Street Archives).
   Pyridine is a chemical substance derived from coal carbonization, recovered most often from coke-oven gases and from coal tar middle oil, and very difficult to work with. (It is usually called "gunk"). However, the world's supply of this material is limited, so it is very expensive.

5. "ACS Heroes of Chemistry Award Honors Seven Dow Ag Veterans", in Around Dow, Dow Company publication, Sept./Oct. 1999.

6. "Midlanders among 'Heroes of Chemistry' award winners", by Don Beckwith, Midland (Mich.) Daily News, Aug. 25, 1999

Chapter 14

1. Much of this chapter is based on oral history, Julius E. Johnson, Sept. 9, 1988, by Terry S. Reynolds, at Post Street Archives, Midland, MI. Also Julius E. Johnson to Keith C. Barrons, nine-page letter re Animal Health Products and other matters, March 30, 2000, at Post Street Archives.

2. Chemically, Zoalene is 3,5-dinitro-ortho-toluamide. See "Zoalene and Coyden", Keith C. Barrons Papers 2-66. For invention of Zoalene see "Growth Company", by E. N. Brandt, p. 167.

3. "Poultry and Farm Animal Disease Control", Barrons Papers 1-20, and "Poultry Disease Control and Nutrition", Barrons Papers 3-86.

4. DNOSBP is dinitro-ortho-secondary-butyl-phenol.

5. See account of this episode in Don Whitehead, The Dow Story, pp. 247-248.

6. OH Julius E. Johnson. See Note 1. above.

7. Julius Johnson, "Life is a Series of Improbabilities", private communication to "Dear Dow Colleague", May 10, 2007.

Chapter 15

1. The main source for this chapter is Oral History, John L. Hagaman, interviewed by the author, May 18, 1992.

2. "Dow and Lilly Complete Formation of Dow Elanco", News & Information Services, The Dow Chemical Company, November 1, 1989.

3. Chemically, trifluralin is 1,1,1-trifluoro-2,6-dinitro-N,N-dipropyl-para-toluidine.

4. Oral history, A. Charles Fischer, interviewed by E. N. Brandt and James J. Bohning, June 8, 2004.

5. It should be noted that as Dow agricultural manager in Japan Hagaman succeeded Robert W. Colby, whom we last met in Chapter 11 as founder of the animal nutrition center in Freeport, Texas.

6. For a fuller account of this dispute and Dow's departure from Korea, see Growth Company, by E. N. Brandt, pp. 490-495.

7. "Agricultural Biotechnology Review Board is Formed", Dow company internal communication, Dow Today No. 57, May 7, 1986.

Chapter 16

1. Much of this chapter is based on Oral History, A. Charles Fischer, interviewed by E. N. Brandt and James J. Bohning, June 8, 2004, at Midland, Michigan.

2. Frank P. Popoff became president and CEO of Dow, 1987-1995. Robert E. Naegele became a member of the Dow board of directors and president of Dow Chemical of Canada.

3. Chlordane, chemically, is 1,2,4,5,6,7,8,8-octachloro-4,7-methano-3a,4,7,7a-tetrahydroindane. The EPA discontinued its use in 1983 except for termite control.

4. In 2000 the EPA honored Dow AgroSciences with its Green Chemistry Challenge Award for spinosad.

5. Silent Spring, by Rachel Carson, Houghton Mifflin Co., Boston, 1962.

6. "Fischer New CEO at Dow AgroSciences", Midland Daily News, March 3, 1999. See also Dow Chemical Company website: http://www.dow.com/aboutdow/lead/fischer.htm, July 27, 2000.

7. Andrew N. Liveris has been president and CEO of the Dow Chemical Company since 2004.

Epilogue

1. See "The Eighth Wonder: American agriculture has done nothing less than feed the world", by Amy L. Fahnestock, in Farm Chemicals, September 1994, 100th Anniversary issue.

2. Ibid.

3. Mike Espy, U.S. Secretary of Agriculture, "Agriculture: America's Greatest Strength", in Farm Chemicals, September 1994.

APPENDIX

ORAL HISTORY INTERVIEWS

(Interviewee, date, location, interviewer(s):

Barnard, Robert D. (Barney), February 21, 1989, Walnut Creek, Calif. (James C. Mackey)
Blair, Etcyl H., May 24, 1994, Midland, Mich. (James J. Bohning and E. N. (Ned) Brandt)
Branch, C. Benson (Ben), November 12, 1988, Houston, Tx. (Bohning), and March 8-9, 1996, Houston, Tx (Holmes H. McClure)
Davidson, John H., June 25, 2002, Midland, Mich. (Brandt)
Downey, Joseph L., June 25, 1998, Midland, Mich. (Bohning and Brandt)
Fischer, A. Charles, June 10, 2004, Midland, Mich. (Bohning and Brandt)
Hagaman, John L., May 18, 1992, Midland, Mich. (Brandt)
Heitz, Robert G., Sept. 26, 1988, Walnut Creek, Calif. (Mackey)
Johnson, Julius E., Sept. 9, 1988, Midland, Mich. (Terry S. Reynolds)
Keil, Robert M., August 8, 1990, MIdland, Mich. (Bohning and Brandt)
Kenaga, Eugene E., May 26, 1994, Midland, Mich. (Bohning and Brandt)
Kociba, Richard,, May 27, 2003, Midland, Mich. (Bohning and Brandt)
Ludwig, Paul D., June 10, 2004, Midland, Mich. (Brandt)
McKennon, Keith R., Dec. 9, 1993, Midland, Mich. (Brandt)
Naegele, Robert E., August 6, 1990, Midland, Mich. (Bohning and Brandt)
Popoff, Frank P., Nov. 16, 1995, Midland, Mich. (Brandt and Arnold Thackray)
Pruitt, Malcolm E., Sept. 9, 1988, Midland, Mich. (Bohning) and March 15, 1996, Lake Jackson, Tx. (McClure)
Rigterink, Raymond H., Oct. 20, 1999, Midland, Mich. (Bohning and Brandt)
Sanford, Donald, October 13, 1983, Brighton, Colorado (Brandt)
Veazey, William R., October 25, 1949, Midland, Mich., (Harrison Hatton)

INDEX

Baron 62

Barrons, Keith C. 1, 2, 50, 54-65, 89, 91, 94
    141, 172, 175

Barstow, E. O. 20

BASF 157

Bayer 195, 210

Bayreuth 101

Beam 156

Beartooth Mountains, 41

Bennett, Earl W. 39, 43, 44

Berkeley 70

Berry, Walter S. (Les) 127

Bexton 143

Billings, Montana 161, 194

Biochemical Research Laboratory 15, 16

Bionetics Laboratory 78

Bioproducts 51, 175

Bizerte 148

Blair, Etcyl H. 3, 96-110, 115, 122, 137

Bohning, James J. 2

Boise, Idoho 194

Bordeaux, France 7

Bordeaux mixture 7, 14

Bordow 14

Boundy, Ray 178

Boyce, Alfred M. 79

Boyce Thompson Institute 121

Brackett, Sterling 169

Brahman 125

Branch, C. Benson 106, 172-4

Brangus 126

Braucher, R. S. (Sid) 79

Brazil 204

Brazoria county 122

Brentwood Cal., 69, 71

Brett, Prof. 132

Brower, Hollis 172, 173

Britton, E. C. 15, 49, 87, 146, 169
Britton, Joseph W. (Bill) 49, 147, 170, 171, 175
Broadstrike 156
Brown, Tom 79
Brown, W. E. (Bill) 73, 169
Brust, Harry 60
Bryant, Clyde 186
Buchanan, Ruth Hale 32, 33
Buchanan, Wiley T. 33
Burpee Seed Co. 62
Buzzelli, David T. 106

-C-

Calcium arsenate 14
Cameron, William J. 34
Campbell, Michael D. 188
Canada 21, 44
Carbon Club 30
Cargill, Inc. 157
Carpenter Street School 114
Carson, Rachel 10, 91, 97, 175, 204
Carter, Walter 82
Carver, George Washington 22-25
Castro, Fidel 61
Catfish 125
Cavanagh, Joe 146
Chemical Heritage Foundation 2
Chemical Industry Institute of Technology (CIIT) 104
Cheminova 157
"chemistry of fire" 100
Chemurgy 34
Chevron 183
Chichester, Lew A. 43
China 9
Chippewa Nature Center 90
Chloracne 98

Chlorophyll 32-34
Chloropicrin 48, 147
Chloropyridines 50
Chlorpyrifos 5
Ciba Geigy 195, 210
Citrus Experiment Station 15
Clorets 33
Coccidiosis 168-169
Colby, Robert W. 122
Colorado University 167
Colorset 149
Columbus, New Mexico 42
Concord 67
Copper Sulfate 22
Costates Mark 156
Costle, Douglas 104, 179
Cote, Elzie 19
Coulter, Llewellyn L. (Bud) 58, 59
Countryman, Mary 79
Courtney, Diane 177
Cox, Winifred 114
Coyden 51-2, 115
Crabgrass killer 50
Crafts, Alden 80
Crummet, Warren 99-100
Cuba 61
Cuero 193
Currie, Gilbert 39
Cutlass 156
Cyanamid 85

-D-

Dacthal 116
Dalapn 6, 49, 50, 58, 59, 60

Daphnia 51, 89
Davidson, John H. 60, 144-152
Davis, Calif. 50, 83
Davis, Clyde 70, 72
Daxtron 51
DDT 12, 17, 48, 62, 86, 147, 168
Denver Colo. 77, 92
Des Moines, Iowa 77
Dieter, Curt 150
Dinoseb 5
Dinitro compounds 15
Dioxin 98
DN-Dust 16, 78-79, 80
DNOCHP 5, 15, 149
Doan, H. D (Ted) 1, 2, 170
Doan, Leland I. 39, 170
Dollar Mountain 72
Double Lazy V 125
Douglas Lake 85
Dowco 41, 155
DowElanco 155, 156, 184, 205
Dowfume 48, 49
Dow General Weed Killer 5, 81
Dow, Grace A. 29
Dow, Herbert H. 117, 155
Downey, Joseph 199
Down to Earth 40
Dowpon 6, 51, 58-59, 60
Dow Selective Weed Killer 5, 48, 81, 147
Dow Spray Dormant 16, 146,
Dow Symphony Orchestra 103
Dow, Willard H. 32
Drake University 77
Drusenheim 185
Dupont de Nemours, E. I. 58, 182
Dupuy, Lee F. 188
Dursban 5, 6, 51, 116, 154, 156, 162, 197

Dutton, Walter 12, 58-59, 145, 146, 171, 173

-E-

-F-

Frolic Sweet Shoppe 114
Fumazone 82, 194
Furches, Barbara J. 188
Fuson, Reynold C. 167

-G-

Gallant 156
Garlon 155, 156, 162
Garvan, Francis P. 35
Gaver, Larry 79
Gehring, Perry 139
Georgetown, British Guyana 131
Gerwick, Ben 156
Glutex 158
Goldman, Lynn 202
Good, Connie 2
Gore, Sen. Albert 104
Goring, Cleve A. I. 2, 130-148, 163
Goulet, Dolores 2
Great Western Electrochemical Co. 70
Green, Hetty 44
Greenville, Miss. 50, 150
Gross, Richard M. (Rick) 164
Gustavson, Reuben G. (Gus) 167

-H-

Hackenberg, Harvey 23
Hagaman, John L. 180-190, 206
Hagaman, Nelda 186
Hale, William J. 28-36
Hamaker, John 134

Hammer, Oscar H. (Trip) 94
Hanson, William R. 48
Harris, Guy 73, 169
Hart Commission Hearings 98
Hart, Sen. Philip 98
Harvard University 31
Hatch, Fred 175
Hawaii 61, 72
Haynes, Willims 35-36
Head, James 133, 134
Heath, Sheldon R. (Ted) 146
Hefner, Robert 141
Heitz, Robert 67, 71, 74
Hemwall, Jack 132
Herculex 157, 158
Herty, Charles H. 34
Hirschkind, W. 70, 71
Hodnett, Prof. 133
Hoechst 210
Holland, Mich. 113
Hong Kong 186
Hope College 113
House Beautiful 63
Hoyle, Harold R. 49
Hummer, Richard W. 88
Hupmobile 67
Hymas, Theo 170, 171, 175

-I-

Illinois Foundation Seeds 157
Imperial Chemical Industries Ltd. (ICI) 211
Indianapolis, Ind. 78, 185
International Joint Commission of the Great Lakes 91
Iodine & Insecticides Div. (I & I) 16, 80
Iowa State College 18, 185

Ireland 9
Irish, Don D. 15, 84, 146, 168

-J-

Jacks, J. V. 10
Japan 187-188
Jellinek, Stephen 105
Jennison Nature Center 90
Johnson grass 61
Johnson, Julius E. 48, 50, 82, 91, 94, 98, 140, 166-179
Johnson, Maxwell 82
Johnson, Steve 204
Johnston, Brian 162
Johnston, Howard 116, 133, 134, 135, 155, 160-165
Johnston, Virginia 163

-K-

Kagy, E. O. 79
Kagy, John F. 1, 15, 16, 48, 76-83, 131-2, 163, 171, 185
Kansas State University 101
Karl, James C. 189
Kedlor 52, 189
Kenaga, Eugene E. 3, 51, 84-94, 116, 121, 177
Kettering, Charles (Boss) 25
King's Lynn, Great Britain 171
Kingston, R.I. 22
Kleschik, William 156
K-List 114
Korea Pacific Chemical Corp. 189
Korlan 87
Kuala Lumpur 60
Kuron 50, 150

Mussell, Dorsey 169
Mycogen 156, 158

-N-

Naegele, Robert E. 139, 195
Napthalene acetic acid 147
National Agricultural Chemicals Association 141, 209
Nation, Hoyt 170
Nelb, Tawny Ryan 2
Nellite 82, 102
Nelson, Sen. Gaylord 197
Nematodes 151
New York Agricultural Experiment station 55
New Zealand 73
Niger 9
Norbak 51
Norris, Jessie 107
North Dakota 58
North Dakota State University 58
Norton, Ted 88
Novege 51
N-Serve 51, 72, 133, 154, 155, 156, 165, 196
Nurelle 156

-O-

Occupational Safety and Health Administration (OSHA) 102
Ohio State University 121, 141
Ohman, M. F. (Fred) 79
Okinawa 86
"Old Farm" 150
Oldershaw, Chuck 67
Oldsmobile 69
Orange, Agent 98

Organic Research Laboratory 15, 114
Osawatomie, Kansas 68
Otis, Chet 60, 140, 171, 178
Ovotran 88
Oxnard, Calif. 48

-P-

Paarlan 156
Palermo 148
Paris, Rupert E. 21
Pearson, Norman 156
Penoxsulam 157
Peribere, Jerome 208
Perkins, Ralph P. 113, 134
Perrin, Eugene E. 49
Pershing, Gen. John J. ("Black Jack") 42
Pertet process 70
Phenol 33, 72
Phyllets 33
Picloram 6, 51,162
Pineapple Research Institute 82
Pitman-Moore 175
Putsburg, Calif. 154, 161
Plictran 52, 88
Polyethylene D 154
Popoff, Frank 195
Post Street Archives 1
Powers, Thomas J. 177
Premerge 48, 147, 172
Prendergast, David T. 79
Presbyterian Church 114
Prochim 155
Prochimagro 155
Pronto 156
Pruitt, Malcolm E. (Mac) 102, 138
Purdue University 113

-Q-

Quarles, John 61
Quonset hut 86

-R-

Radapon 6
Ralston-Purina 171, 185
Ranger, Texas 185
Raynor, Dick 171
Reading, University of 137
Redemann, Carl 134-5
Red Lodge, Montana 41
Reifschneider, Walter 161-2
Reldan 156-7
Reno, Nevada 71
Rhode Island Agricultural Experiment Station 22
Rhone Pulence 182, 210
Ribicoff, Sen. Abraham 176
Richardson, A. P. 169
Richardson, C. H. 78
Richmond, Calif. 72
Richmond, Virginia 32
Riecker, Margaret A. (Ranny) 2
Rigterink, Leta 113
Rigterink, Raymond 112-119
Ripper, Walter 60, 172
Riverside, Calif. 79
Roberts, Donna J. 103
Roberts, Edward R. 182
Rockefeller Foundation 167
Rohm & Haas 153
Ronnel 87, 102, 124
Rooke, David L. 105, 142

Roosevelt, Theodore 23
Rose, William C. 167
Rotary Club 26
Rothamsted 136-7
Roundup 210
Rowe, V. K. 104, 177
Rubigan 156
Ruckelshaus, William 179
Ruelene 51, 102, 116, 123
Ruh, Robert 87
Russia 9

-S-

Sacramento, Calif. 49, 83
Sadat, Anwar 104
Safety Dept. 16
Salisbury Laboratories 169
Sanford, Don 15, 38-46
San Francisco 70
Sao Paulo 200
Schistosomiasis 89
Scott, Ellen 121
Seal Beach, Calif. 16, 48, 50, 131, 162, 171, 185
Sentrachem 156
Sentricon 157
Shah Alam 60
Shelby, Mich 145
Shell 85, 149
Sirlene 51
Smith, Hillard 60, 61, 194
Smith, Len 164
Society of Environmental Toxicology and Chemistry
(SETAC) 93
Sodium benzonate 1, 20-24
Sodium TCA 59
Sonalan 156

Thorne, Gerald 81
Thorpe's Dictionary of Applied Chemistry 22
Tobigo Lagoon 90
Togwatee Pass 69
Tolksmith, Henry 87
Torndon 6, 8, 51, 77, 133, 135, 154, 155, 156, 157, 162, 201
Tracer 156, 157, 203
Traverse City, Mich, 65
Treflan 156, 183
Trichloracetic acid 58
Trifluralin 183, 196
Trimidal 156
Trolene 102
Tucker, Richard E. 93
Turflon 156
Turner, Georgge 134
"Two-a-day Ray" 118, 2,
4-D 55-59, 61, 150-1
2, 4, 5-T 58, 150, 154

-U-

Underhill, Robert 79
Union Carbine Corp. 157, 183
United States Department of Agriculture 6, 20, 137
United States Department of Interior 92
United States Fish & Wildlife Service 92
United States Trade Mark Office 6
University of California 16, 79
University of California at Berkeley 162
University of Goettingen 31
University of Illinois 91, 167
University of Kansas 185
University of Michigan 85
University of Ohio at Athens 121

University of Tennessee 168
University of Wyoming 68

-V-

Valbonne 205
Veazey, W. R. 15, 41
Valasquez, Jenee 2
Verdict 155-6
Verdurin Company 33
Verett, Jacqueline 98
Vietnam 62, 194
Vikane 72,156
Villa, Pancho 42-3
Villars, Charles 118-9

-W-

Wageningen University, Holland 136
Wall Street Journal 63
Walnut Creek, Calif. 83
Washington, Booker T. 22-3
Watson, Andrew J. 60, 151
Weed Society of America 6, 152
West Branch, Mich. 34
Westbury, Christina (Chrissy) 2
Wheeler, H. J. 21-2
White, Agent 162
Whittier, Calif. 48, 81
Wiley Harvey W. 20-1, 23
Williams, Clayton S. 184
Willow Pass 67
Winfield, Kansas 101
Wittenberg College 121

Wolfe, Sidney 101
World Health Organization 89, 92
Wynona, Okla. 101
Wyoming 68

-X-Y-

Yellowstone National Park 42, 69
Yonkers, New York 121
Young, Boyd 121
Youngson, C. R. (Dick) 82, 132

-Z-

Zectran 143
Zeneca 157, 210
Zoalene 50, 73, 170, 171
Zoamix 50, 169
Zytron 102, 116